THE BOOK

OF

TAWHID

Nine Discourses
given between March 27th
and May 29th 2004
at Al-Jami'a Mosque,
Claremont, Cape Town

Copyright © The Dallas Foundation, 2022 CE/1443 AH

The Book of Tawhid

Published by:	Diwan Press Ltd.
	311 Allerton Road
	Bradford
	BD15 7HA
	UK
Website:	www.diwanpress.com
E-mail:	info@diwanpress.com

Author: Shaykh Dr. Abdalqadir as-Sufi

A catalogue record of this book is available from the British Library.

978-1-914397-15-8 (casebound)
978-1-914397-21-9 (paperback)

PREFACE

Due to the interregnum, soon, inshallah, to be brought
to an end, which marks the period from which Islamic
governance was interrupted, that is to say in the Mughal
and Osmanli Dawlets, we, the Muslim World Community, experience Islam without its utterly necessary dimension of political command. One oddly regrettable result
of this has been that we have started to take our Imams
as leaders, making them into a priesthood, and allowing
them to rule us like a slave population, which, having no
power over either war or wealth, allow themselves to be
commanded in the private matters of births, marriages
and deaths. In this sense our Muslim population have
taken on the form of a totally different religion, Shi'ism.
The proof of this is that we have allowed the kuffar to

define us as belonging to "Sunni Islam", as if accepting
their definition that the Islamic religion has historically
been split into two sects. There can only be one Deen al-
Haqq, and it has Divine authorisation to be called Islam.
Allah the Exalted says in Surat al-Ma'ida (5:3):

اَلْيَوْمَ يَئِسَ الَّذِينَ كَفَرُوا مِنْ دِينِكُمْ فَلَا
تَخْشَوْهُمْ وَاخْشَوْنِ اِلْيَوْمَ اَكْمَلْتُ لَكُمْ دِينَكُمْ وَأَتْمَمْتُ عَلَيْكُمْ
نِعْمَتِي وَرَضِيتُ لَكُمُ الاِسْلَامَ دِينًا

Today the kuffar have despaired of overcoming your deen.
So do not be afraid of them but be afraid of Me.
Today I have perfected your deen for you
and completed My blessing upon you
and I am pleased with Islam as a deen for you.

Another result of this is, that in treating the Imam as an
Authority, rather than that utterly replaceable figure
whose noble task is to lead the Salat, the members of the
Jama'at have lost that dynamic relationship with the text
of the Qur'an on which a vibrant Islamic community
has to be founded. In our books of Seerat and Hadith we
find that the Sahaba used to gather after Fajr, and those
among them who knew some Qur'an would recite it,
after which they would reflect in order to see how they
could apply its guidance to the day's affairs.

It was in that spirit that we decided to hold a series of
gatherings in order to give a start to this dynamic relationship between the Jama'at and the Book of Allah. In

reviving this Madinan 'Amal, it was only fitting that we should begin the matter by extracting from the Qur'an itself the clear explications of Allah, glory be to Him, about Himself, that is, the knowledge of Tawhid.

So it was that in these nine gatherings, each one of the Fuqara, men and women, sat with the Qur'an in front of them, and at every reference to the Qur'an in the text which follows, the Jama'at would themselves look up the Ayats, and they would also be recited by our Hafidh. As a result, by the end of the study series the group felt at home with handling the Qur'an, looking it up, and finding the Surat and the Ayat. One could say that the Jama'at, in this small event, had recovered for themselves the Clear Book which had, after all, been sent down from Allah, glory be to Him, for them, and not just some priestly class who used it to assure them a living, to take it out in the rituals of birth, marriage and death, and even, astaghfirullah, hold it over the householder's head when he left the house on a journey!

One could add a further result to this matter. It is precisely this Jama'at that has most fully grasped that the paid Imams (a Makruh situation in the Shari'at) have neither taught, nor called for, nor activated the need for a community to be governed by an Amir, and that the Amir, in turn, must impose with his Zakat Collectors that collected Zakat without which there simply is no Islam at all.

Shaykh Dr. Abdalqadir as-Sufi

I

MARCH 27TH 2004

We will Look at Surat al-Ahzab (33:34-35).

وَاذْكُرْنَ مَا يُتْلَىٰ فِي بُيُوتِكُنَّ
مِنْ ءَايَٰتِ ٱللَّهِ وَٱلْحِكْمَةِ إِنَّ ٱللَّهَ كَانَ لَطِيفًا خَبِيرًا ۝
إِنَّ ٱلْمُسْلِمِينَ وَٱلْمُسْلِمَٰتِ وَٱلْمُؤْمِنِينَ وَٱلْمُؤْمِنَٰتِ وَٱلْقَٰنِتِينَ
وَٱلْقَٰنِتَٰتِ وَٱلصَّٰدِقِينَ وَٱلصَّٰدِقَٰتِ وَٱلصَّٰبِرِينَ
وَٱلصَّٰبِرَٰتِ وَٱلْخَٰشِعِينَ وَٱلْخَٰشِعَٰتِ وَٱلْمُتَصَدِّقِينَ
وَٱلْمُتَصَدِّقَٰتِ وَٱلصَّٰئِمِينَ وَٱلصَّٰئِمَٰتِ وَٱلْحَٰفِظِينَ
فُرُوجَهُمْ وَٱلْحَٰفِظَٰتِ وَٱلذَّٰكِرِينَ ٱللَّهَ كَثِيرًا
وَٱلذَّٰكِرَٰتِ أَعَدَّ ٱللَّهُ لَهُم مَّغْفِرَةً وَأَجْرًا عَظِيمًا ۝

And remember the Signs of Allah
and the wise words
which are recited in your rooms.
Allah is All-Pervading, All-Aware.

Men and women who are Muslims,
men and women who are muminun,
men and women who are obedient,
men and women who are truthful,
men and women who are steadfast,
men and women who are humble,
men and women who give sadaqa,
men and women who fast,
men and women who guard their private parts,
men and women who remember Allah much:
Allah has prepared forgiveness for them
and an immense reward.

Regarding "Men and women who remember Allah much," the Arabic term used there is "Dhikr." It is "Men and women who do dhikr of Allah," men and women who do the act of remembering.

وَالذَّاكِرِينَ ٱللَّهَ كَثِيرًا
وَٱلذَّاكِرَاتِ أَعَدَّ ٱللَّهُ لَهُم مَّغْفِرَةً وَأَجْرًا عَظِيمًا ۝

Men and women who remember Allah much:
Allah has prepared forgiveness for them
and an immense reward.

Here we have the statement that is the defining ayat of the fuqara and the faqirat, this ayat defines them.

وَاذْكُرْنَ مَا يُتْلَى فِي بُيُوتِكُنَّ
مِنْ ءَايَـٰتِ اللَّهِ وَالْحِكْمَةِ إِنَّ اللَّهَ كَانَ لَطِيفًا خَبِيرًا ۝

And remember the Signs of Allah
and the wise words
which are recited in your rooms.
Allah is All-Pervading, All-Aware.

So Allah, subhanahu wa ta'ala, mentions the worship that you do – not in the mosque – but the worship that you do privately, and He begins in this ayat from that. This already distinguishes these muminun and muminat who have a special place with Allah, subhanahu wa ta'ala.

وَاذْكُرْنَ مَا يُتْلَى فِي بُيُوتِكُنَّ
مِنْ ءَايَـٰتِ اللَّهِ وَالْحِكْمَةِ إِنَّ اللَّهَ كَانَ لَطِيفًا خَبِيرًا ۝

And remember the Signs of Allah
and the wise words
which are recited in your rooms.
Allah is All-Pervading, All-Aware.

"Buyut" here has been translated as "rooms", and that is interesting because if you go to Surat an-Nur (24:36):

$$\text{فِى بُيُوتٍ اَذِنَ اللَّهُ أَن تُرْفَعَ}$$
$$\text{وَيُذْكَرَ فِيهَا اسْمُهُ يُسَبِّحُ لَهُ فِيهَا بِالْغُدُوِّ وَالْاصَالِ ۝}$$

The translation is: "In houses which Allah has permitted to be built," but it is not so much 'houses' – you could almost say zawiyyas. It is the place where people have set themselves apart to do dhikr of Allah, subhanahu wa ta'ala.

Now Allah specifies the spiritual, ruhani qualities of these special people in the next ayat:

$$\text{اِنَّ الْمُسْلِمِينَ وَالْمُسْلِمَاتِ وَالْمُؤْمِنِينَ وَالْمُؤْمِنَاتِ وَالْقَانِتِينَ}$$
$$\text{وَالْقَانِتَاتِ وَالصَّادِقِينَ وَالصَّادِقَاتِ وَالصَّابِرِينَ}$$
$$\text{وَالصَّابِرَاتِ وَالْخَاشِعِينَ وَالْخَاشِعَاتِ وَالْمُتَصَدِّقِينَ}$$
$$\text{وَالْمُتَصَدِّقَاتِ وَالصَّائِمِينَ وَالصَّائِمَاتِ وَالْحَافِظِينَ}$$
$$\text{فُرُوجَهُمْ وَالْحَافِظَاتِ وَالذَّاكِرِينَ اللَّهَ كَثِيرًا}$$
$$\text{وَالذَّاكِرَاتِ أَعَدَّ اللَّهُ لَهُمْ مَغْفِرَةً وَأَجْرًا عَظِيمًا ۝}$$

> Men and women who are Muslims,
> men and women who are muminun,
> men and women who are obedient,
> men and women who are truthful,
> men and women who are steadfast,
> men and women who are humble,
> men and women who give sadaqa,

I

men and women who fast,
men and women who guard their private parts,
men and women who remember Allah much:
Allah has prepared forgiveness for them
and an immense reward.

So Allah, subhanahu wa ta'ala, has meant that for these people, there is something prepared for them. They have a reward. This group of people have the reward with Allah, subhanahu wa ta'ala. They have forgiveness and a vast reward. What would be the vast reward after forgiveness? For the common people it would be like the bill being paid. But there is more than that, there is a vast reward. With Allah, subhanahu wa ta'ala, there is only one thing that would be fitting for the people He has defined and that would be Ma'rifa. The reward of Allah, subhanahu wa ta'ala, is Ma'rifa.

The Arabic word for reward is 'ajra'. This word comes again and again in the Qur'an, and it is to do with this contract Allah has made with the special muminun, the ones who are picked out, the ones who are elevated, and this is the vast reward.

Now we look at Surat al-'Ankabut (29:45):

اتْلُ مَآ أُوحِيَ إِلَيْكَ مِنَ الْكِتَـٰبِ
وَأَقِمِ الصَّلَوٰةَ إِنَّ الصَّلَوٰةَ تَنْهَىٰ عَنِ الْفَحْشَآءِ وَالْمُنكَرِ
وَلَذِكْرُ اللَّهِ أَكْبَرُ وَاللَّهُ يَعْلَمُ مَا تَصْنَعُونَ ۞

Recite what has been revealed to you of the Book
and establish Salat.
Salat precludes indecency and wrongdoing.
And remembrance of Allah is greater still.
Allah knows what you do.

$$ اَتْلُ مَآ أُوحِىَ إِلَيْكَ مِنَ ٱلْكِتَٰبِ وَأَقِمِ ٱلصَّلَوٰةَ $$

Recite what has been revealed to you of the Book
and establish Salat.

So the first order is the recitation of Qur'an. Allah, subhanahu wa ta'ala, puts the two together because the Salat
implies the recitation of Qur'an, thus it is really one
thing. This, again, is the command to Salat which has
built into it the recitation of the Book. There are three
stages, and this is the first stage. The next stage is:

$$ إِنَّ ٱلصَّلَوٰةَ نَنْهِىٰ عَنِ ٱلْفَحْشَآءِ وَٱلْمُنْكَرِ $$

Salat precludes indecency and wrongdoing.

Having established that, Allah then puts another level on
to constructing the complete human being. The next
level is, "Salat precludes indecency and wrongdoing," so
the moral behaviour cannot be imposed on him if you
have not already established the recitation of Qur'an,
and the Salat. Then you can impose on man the correct
moral behaviour. It is as if the kuffar, who are nowadays
attacking Islam, were saying that we are harsh with
people, and in fact you could say that people in Arabia
are harsh with their own people because they have not

established the recitation of Qur'an which leads to the understanding of its meaning, and the Salat – so then they can ask of their people to have a moral behaviour and if they do not, with that situation the Shari'ah is there to put the limits on human behaviour. Human behaviour has to be limited, otherwise man will go to the extremes of destruction.

$$وَلَذِكْرُ اللَّهِ أَكْبَرُ$$

And remembrance of Allah is greater still.

So the highest aspect of this is that you are now another type of human being. You are people who make Salat, who worship Allah with the knowledge of the words of Qur'an, and therefore you have taken on this correct behaviour – but greater is the dhikr of Allah. So that which gives you access to Ma'rifatullah is the highest aspect of the human being. Then we come to the inescapable reality of the Muslim situation:

$$وَاللَّهُ يَعْلَمُ مَا تَصْنَعُونَ ۝$$

Allah knows what you do.

The dynamic of this superior being, the Muslim – that is superior to the kuffar – is that he knows that Allah knows what he does. This is another kind of being. The Wird as-Sahl, of the great Sufi of the East, Sahl at-Tustari was from Qur'an:

$$الله معي الله ناظر إلي الله شاهد علي$$

Allah is with me, Allah sees me,
Allah is the Witness of my acts.

This is what made him have direct experience, ‘Ilm al-laduni, of Allah, subhanahu wa ta’ala.

Now we go to Surat al-Baqara (2:152):

فَاذْكُرُونِيٓ أَذْكُرْكُمْ وَاشْكُرُواْ لِى وَلَا تَكْفُرُونِ ۝

Remember Me – I will remember you.
Give thanks to Me and do not be ungrateful.

This ayat is an ayat ‘adhim because this is a very high thing that Allah is telling the muminun. Look at the construction:

فَاذْكُرُونِيٓ

Remember Me,

أَذْكُرْكُمْ

I will remember you.

It has exactly the same construct but is like a mirror image of it. It is like saying "If we remember Him, He remembers us" – and the Sufis say, "Who is the remem-berer?" Allah, subhanahu wa ta’ala, says, "Remember Me and I remember you." So the lover becomes the beloved. Who is the lover and who is the beloved? This is the secret, this is the very heart of what can be spoken,

because beyond that you cannot say. But Allah, subhanahu wa ta'ala, has openly said in the Qur'an that the lover
is the beloved and the beloved is the lover. "Remember
Me – I will remember You." Love Me and I will love you.

Let us look now at Surat al-Muzzammil (73:8-9):

وَاذْكُرِ اسْمَ رَبِّكَ وَتَبَتَّلْ إِلَيْهِ تَبْتِيلاً ۝ رَبُّ الْمَشْرِقِ
وَالْمَغْرِبِ لَا إِلَهَ إِلَّا هُوَ فَاتَّخِذْهُ وَكِيلاً ۝

Remember the Name of your Lord,
and devote yourself to Him completely.
Lord of the East and West –
there is no god but Him –
so take Him as your Guardian.

This is the command. This is what runs through the
Qur'an. Remember that the Qur'an is full of very feroc-
ious things, terrible things – it is full of these warnings
to the kuffar about the Fire, about the destruction of cit-
ies, about the punishment of Allah, about how He will
not allow these deviations of the human beings and how
in every age He has smashed them. But then underneath
this running all the time is this message to the
muminun: "Allah has prepared forgiveness for them and
an immense reward." This is what you have to do. This
is your business. "Remember the Name of your Lord."
Dhikr is the order on these ones who are the elite, and
the elite of the elite is to be people who live in dhikr.
They are created for dhikr because Allah, subhanahu wa
ta'ala, says in Surat adh-Dhariyat (51:56):

$$وَمَا خَلَقْتُ ٱلْجِنَّ وَالْإِنسَ إِلَّا لِيَعْبُدُونِ ۝٥٦﴾$$

I only created jinn and man to worship Me.

This is the order from Allah. This is what you are created for, and is what only these special people have understood.

$$وَاذْكُرِ اسْمَ رَبِّكَ وَتَبَتَّلْ إِلَيْهِ تَبْتِيلًا ۝﴾$$

Remember the Name of your Lord,
and devote yourself to Him completely.

Allah, subhanahu wa ta'ala, says: "Devote yourself to Him completely," which means you do nothing else! The people who did not have the Sirat al-Mustaqim would think therefore that they had to go up into a mountain and stand on one leg, and that they had to shut themselves off from the world in order to do this thing. But Allah, subhanahu wa ta'ala, explains in Surat al-'Imran (3:191):

$$الَّذِينَ يَذْكُرُونَ اللَّهَ قِيَامًا وَقُعُودًا وَعَلَىٰ جُنُوبِهِمْ﴾$$

...those who remember Allah, standing,
sitting and lying on their sides.

This means that in every situation you remember Allah. Also Allah, subhanahu wa ta'ala, says in Surat an-Nur (24:37):

$$رِجَالٌ لَّا تُلْهِيهِمْ تِجَارَةٌ وَلَا بَيْعٌ عَن ذِكْرِ اللَّهِ﴾$$

Men who are not distracted by trade or commerce
from the remembrance of Allah.

So trading, doing business, does not distract you from
the remembrance of Allah. So this order: "Devote yourself to Him completely," means that you live in the Presence of Allah, the Hadrat ar-Rabbani in every situation.

If you look at the Diwan of Shaykh Muhammad ibn al-
Habib, radiyallahu 'anhu, he says that the thing which
stands in your way is your nafs. If you remember yourself, you are forgetting Allah. Surat al-'Asr (103):

$$\text{بِسْمِ اللهِ الرَّحْمَنِ الرَّحِيمِ}$$
$$\text{وَالْعَصْرِ ۝ إِنَّ الْإِنسَانَ لَفِي خُسْرٍ ۝ إِلَّا الَّذِينَ ءَامَنُوا}$$
$$\text{وَعَمِلُوا الصَّالِحَاتِ وَتَوَاصَوْا بِالْحَقِّ وَتَوَاصَوْا بِالصَّبْرِ ۝}$$

In the name of Allah, All-Merciful, Most Merciful
By the Late Afternoon, truly man is in loss –
except for those who have Iman and do right actions
and urge each other to the truth
and urge each other to steadfastness.

So man is in forgetfulness and what he is forgetful of is
the reality of his own existence. He owes his existence to
Allah. His existence is evidence of Allah, and he forgets!
And Allah says: "When you forget, remember."

Now we look at part of Ayat 165 in Surat al-Baqara:

$$وَالَّذِينَ ءَامَنُوٓا أَشَدُّ حُبًّا لِلَّهِ$$

But those who have Iman have greater love for Allah.

So Allah, subhanahu wa ta'ala, is placing a certain group of the humans higher because they have greater love of Allah, subhanahu wa ta'ala. This is a qualitative difference. All men are not equal. With Allah they are not the same. There is no equality, because there is a portion of the human race who are the muminun, who are pleasing to Allah, and who have a greater love for Allah, and this places them higher.

Look now at Surat al-'Imran (3:31):

$$قُلْ إِن كُنتُمْ تُحِبُّونَ اللَّهَ فَاتَّبِعُونِي يُحْبِبْكُمُ اللَّهُ وَيَغْفِرْ لَكُمْ ذُنُوبَكُمْ ۗ وَاللَّهُ غَفُورٌ رَّحِيمٌ ۝$$

Say, "If you love Allah, then follow me
and Allah will love you and forgive you
for your wrong actions.
Allah is Ever-Forgiving, Most Merciful."

Now is revealed the whole process by which this happens, because it begins with this vital word in Qur'an which is 'Qul'. This means that it is a command from Allah from the angel to Rasul.

Now we get the whole story: "Say, 'If you love Allah, then follow me.'" So Rasul is ordering the people, "If you love Allah, then follow me." You cannot love Allah and

I

not follow Rasul. This means we have no dialogue with other religions. There is nothing to say to other religions. If you love Allah then you have to follow Rasul – finished! That is the end of our dialogue – go back, go away! If you really love Allah then you will follow Rasul, sallallahu 'alayhi wa sallam.

This is an order from Allah where He says: "Say!" Sallallahu 'alayhi wa sallam is not saying it from himself, he is saying it under the Divine imperative.

قُلْ إِن كُنتُمْ تُحِبُّونَ ٱللَّهَ فَٱتَّبِعُونِى يُحْبِبْكُمُ ٱللَّهُ وَيَغْفِرْ لَكُمْ ذُنُوبَكُمْ وَٱللَّهُ غَفُورٌ رَّحِيمٌ ۝

Say, 'If you love Allah, then follow me
and Allah will love you and forgive you
for your wrong actions.
Allah is Ever-Forgiving, Most Merciful.'

The Prophet's order is to tell the people that if they love Allah, they have to follow the Rasul. Then Allah will love them, which means, again, in this contract which we have taken, that if Allah loves the mumin then the lover becomes the beloved. Then the door is open to Ma'rifatullah. Once the sentence is read, that is Ma'rifa. There is no other way that you can go. You have now reached the point where you have available to you Ma'rifatullah.

"Allah will love you" means that you love Allah so that you follow Rasul, sallallahu 'alayhi wa sallam, and you have Ma'rifa of Allah, subhanahu wa ta'ala. And you are forgiven for your wrong actions. In other words, the life-term is wiped out, the whole thing is gone. Then you are told:

$$وَاللَّهُ غَفُورٌ رَّحِيمٌ ۝$$

Allah is Ever-Forgiving, Most Merciful.

About this matter which we have been looking at: first of all, it is like the Qur'an has one aspect for everybody because the Book is revealed for the whole world. So there are a few places in the Book where Allah, subhanahu wa ta'ala, says, "Ya ayyuhann-Nas." He speaks to mankind because there is always the possibility among these millions and millions of people that there would be one who hears the message.

Then Allah, subhanahu wa ta'ala, warns with tremendous warnings which are terrifying. He says, "Ya ayyuhal-Kafirun" – to the kafirun this is going to happen, make no mistake about it. There is the inevitability that the darkness of that inner life will in the next world have a punishment which will be a torment greater than the torment they had in this world.

Then He says, "Ya ayyuhalladhina amanu," and he speaks to the muminun and gives them guidance. Then he tells them that He has set up the people on different levels, and He has mentioned, as we saw in the Surat al-Waqi'a, the Muqarrabun, the people who come near. He has now revealed this whole structure for the access to Ma'rifa.

You might think that this is not in the Qur'an, but these

ayats are embedded like jewels among the other decorations and beauties of the Qur'an. That is that Allah, subhanahu wa ta'ala, talks about Ma'rifa. He talks about love in a very high and exalted way which is connected to direct knowledge. There is a knowledge that is not information, there is a knowledge that is illumination – 'Ilm al-laduni, direct from Allah, subhanahu wa ta'ala.

One of the shuyukh of the East made a very similar description to Imam al-Ghazali's, radiyallahu 'anhu. He said that this love has ten stages. The first is Muwafaqa – Compatibility. The way of having this compatibility with Allah, subhanahu wa ta'ala, is to regard the enemies of the Beloved as our enemies, and His friends as our friends. So right at the beginning he makes this division that is in the Qur'an: Do not take the kafirun as your friends. You separate yourself from them and regard the enemies of the Beloved as our enemies and the friends of the Beloved, of Allah, subhanahu wa ta'ala, as our friends.

The next is Mayyal – Inclination. The heart is an instrument and the heart begins to move. The word for heart in Arabic is 'qalb' from the root QLB which means to turn over. So the heart is always turning over, it is always in motion. It is like that part of the steering of a ship or submarine which is like a fulcrum that is always turning. So the heart will always go to something, and if it does not go to the halal it will go to the haram, and if it wants the haram it will get the haram because it is like a magnet – if it wants the bad it will get the bad, if it wants the good it will get the good. If it wants food, then the food is coming to it, and the secret of understanding the destiny is that the food is coming to you before you get hungry. It is actually on its way! It was a sheep in a field which has been slaughtered, and then it has been hung, and then sent to the butcher's, it has been bought, it has been taken to the kitchen – you think, "I'm hungry," and there it is on the plate in front of you. The Awliya say that this meal has been coming to you from before the creation of the world, because Allah is the Provider. The rizq is from the Razzaq.

This is the first movement of the heart. First you are compatible, you are in tune with the Beloved because you have learned not to like the enemies of Allah. That makes you compatible, it makes you acceptable. Then comes inclination, and this is to busy yourself on your quest for the Beloved. In other words, your heart begins to ask, "Why is it so difficult? What do I do? What should I do? How am I to move about? How am I to have knowledge? How is it that I sit through the dhikr and am not having something happen inside me?" and the heart begins to incline.

Then the next stage is Muanasa – Fellowship. The heart begins to want to be with the people who love Allah because one of the signs of the lovers is that they love to hear the name of the Beloved. It is like the story of Layla and Majnun. It is enough for Majnun to hear the name of Layla that he is happy. So he wants to go where her name is said. The beginning of Muanasa is to attach yourself to Allah sincerely and to detach yourself from everything else. The way you detach yourself from everything else is by beginning to get into the habit of sitting with the people who love Allah, subhanahu wa ta'ala.

Then this closeness begins to take on a dynamic. The next stage is Hawa – Passion. But this passion is the opposite of the passion of the world, it is to keep the heart in zuhd. In other words, not to let it have anything except the passion for the dhikr, for the Presence of Allah, for the knowledge of Allah. So with this, the heart begins to become certain, it begins to become pliable, it begins to become accessible to things it was not accessible to before. That is the explanation of the famous sentence of Imam al-Ghazali, radiyallahu 'anhu: "The person who has put one foot on the path is like a star. The one who is advanced on the path is like a moon. The one who has achieved knowledge of Allah is like the sun. But the one who has not put one foot on the path is like a stone."

The fifth stage is Muwadda – Friendship. What makes the friendship with Allah is that before anything else the dominant experience of the heart is yearning. So you are reaching beyond the business of living. You have a yearning that reaches out past everything to do with 'thing'. Shaykh Muhammad ibn al-Habib, rahimahullah, says in the Diwan,

$$\text{وَغِبْ فِيهِ عَـنْ سِوَاهُ}$$

Withdraw yourself in Him
from all that is other-than Him.

The sixth stage is Khulla – Exclusive Friendship. You book in not just your intellect and your heart, but you book in all the limbs of the body to be in this condition. This is what Salat is for, this is what fasting is for, and this is what the imara is for – that the limbs of the body become worshipful.

The seventh stage is Mahabba – Affection. Mahabba is that the intensity of this longing and love and desire begins to burn up in the faqir the things which are no good, the things which are not right. They just galvanise and in their place comes the possibility of doing good actions. You move from being concerned with yourself, which brings about bad actions, to not being concerned about yourself but having compassion for others, because this love spills out into a love for the fuqara. It spills out, it overflows so that your body overflows to take in all the people and you do not know which is you and which is them. This is because you then have taken on good actions. Living in good actions, in what is called birr – birr is active, it is not just goodness, but that you are actively doing good.

Then you come to the eighth stage which is Shaghaf – Violent Affection. So the intensity increases and the Shaghaf becomes so that you are so intoxicated that you are liable, as he says, "To risk tearing the veil of your secret," because to disclose the secret is like kufr. In other words, in the dhikr you become so intoxicated that you might reveal this knowledge which is coming into your heart of Allah, subhanahu wa ta'ala, yet no-one must know. Shaykh Muhammad ibn al-Habib says in his Diwan:

$$\text{وَاذْكُرْ بِجِدٍّ وَصِدْقٍ} \quad \text{بَيْنَ يَـدَيْ عَبِيدِ اللّٰه}$$

I

> Do dhikr with gravity and sincerity
> in front of the slaves of Allah.

The Ninth stage is Taym – Enslavement. You become a captive slave of love, and that is to put on tajrid which is to strip away. There are two tajrids: there is the tajrid of the outward which is to do without, like zuhd. Zuhd is not, "I won't have it," it is "I don't need it." Imam al-Ghazali tells of Sayyiduna 'Isa, 'alayhi salam, having a comb and a mirror. He saw a child running its hands through its hair and he threw away the comb. Then he saw the animal go to the water, and realised that if you look into the water you can see yourself, so he threw away the mirror.

This is outward tajrid, but the inner tajrid is to strip away the body itself. In the khalwa there is a tajrid of the batin which is that you lose the hearing, the sight, the touch – you lose all the senses one by one, so that what is left is a consciousness which in its turn vanishes which is, in the language of Tasawwuf, 'Fana fillah'. One of the Sufis said about Taym, about this enslavement: "You wish to buy Him – first sell yourself." This is the counsel of the 'Arif to the one who wants this knowledge.

The tenth stage is Walah – Bewilderment. Muhiyuddin Ibn al-'Arabi has written many things about Walah. This shaykh says it is, "To place the mirror of the heart before the Beloved to be intoxicated in the wine of beauty." There is another of these shaykhs – Yahya al-Muniri, who said, "Love (hubb) sends a message from the Beloved, and the message to the heart is: 'Be always in motion, restless.'

To life: 'Let go of joys.' To the head: 'Do not settle.' To the face: 'Lose your complexion.' To the body: 'Say goodbye to vanishing strength.' To the eyes: 'Shed tears,' and to the lover himself: 'Hide your condition. Shut your mouth. Pull back from friends. Get rid of both the worlds.'"

II

April 3rd 2004

Last week we were looking in the Qur'an at the use and presentation by Allah, subhanahu wa ta'ala, of one word, 'Hubb' – the love of Allah, subhanahu wa ta'ala, and the meanings of this love for the muminun.

Tonight we look at the meanings of one other word which is 'ibada. We will look at what defines 'ibada, which is that the way in which the mumin aligns himself with worship of Allah, subhanahu wa ta'ala, this 'ibada is from 'abd. So the worship of Allah, subhanahu wa ta'ala, is itself slavehood. It is putting oneself under the acknowledgement of the power of Allah, subhanahu wa ta'ala, and it is from the knowledge in which the 'ibada is performed that it takes its meaning.

There is a very famous hadith in the Sahih collection which recurs in various versions, where Rasul, sallallahu 'alayhi wa sallam, in defining the importance of Salat refers to a Salat with understanding. This is not the same as someone just going through the motions of Salat, but it is someone who knows what this standing, bowing and prostrating means. Who is being worshipped is what gives it meaning. This is what we will look at in the following ayats.

Look at Surat Al 'Imran (3:175), the second part of the ayat:

$$\text{فَلَا تَخَافُوهُمْ وَخَافُونِ إِن كُنتُم مُّؤْمِنِينَ ﴿١٧٥﴾}$$

But do not fear them – fear Me if you are muminun.

The word khawf is fear, actual fear. It is not a psychological condition, but physical. Khawf is what goes through the body, like the man seeing the wild tiger. Allah, subhanahu wa ta'ala, says, "Do not fear them – fear Me if you are muminun," so Allah is taking the mumin and changing his whole identity so that 'them' in this general sense refers to the enemy, and it therefore also refers to everything in the creation that the mumin is afraid of. Do not be afraid of what opposes you and what confronts you, but "fear Me," fear Allah, subhanahu wa ta'ala.

Here He is using a structure by which He says, "Me," and when Allah, subhanahu wa ta'ala, says that, it is as though He is speaking from His Essence because He is speaking about Himself in the first person. Sometimes He speaks in the Qur'an to the people about Himself as 'He', but here He is saying 'Me,' so this is an absolute command from the very core of our understanding of Allah, subhanahu wa ta'ala.

"Fear Me if you are muminun." In other words, the condition of being mumin, of being one who trusts in Allah, is that he has fear of Allah. Fear of Allah means that you cannot have fear of anything else. It is a change in the condition of the human creature who has become mumin, and at this point the fear that he would have of the other, and of the enemy, and of what opposes him, this khawf becomes something very deep that is fear of Allah, subhanahu wa ta'ala. That in itself would be so great that it would paralyse the mumin if it were the only condition under which he could live, and great Awliya have had such a great fear of Allah, subhanahu wa ta'ala, at a certain stage of their journey to Allah that they have become transfixed by it and Allah, by His power, has taken them out of that and this is because in the language of Tasawwuf, khawf is balanced against raja', hope.

There is a famous story of the man who came to Shaykh Muhammad ibn al-Habib, rahimahullah, from the Sahara to give him the Idhn of being in the Darqawi Tariqa. Shaykh Muhammad ibn al-Habib, rahimahullah, was then teaching Arabic in the Qarawiyyin mosque in Fes, and this man had been sent with an instruction from his shaykh: "Go to the Qarawiyyin and when you get there, there will be a circle of 'ulama sitting. Go up to

them and say, 'I am the guest of Allah'," which is a way
of asking for hospitality, "and whoever accepts, you go
with that man."

So this man, who was one of the salihun, went there and
said, "I am the guest of Allah," and they all bowed their
heads, they did not want the bother of this guest from
the Sahara. "I am the guest of Allah." The third time he
asked, Shaykh Muhammad ibn al-Habib, rahimahullah,
said, "Marhaban," and took him.

He took him to a tiny little room he had in the wall of
Fes. The room is built inside the wall and so the steps up
are very steep. As he climbed the steps, this man who had
been sent to Shaykh Muhammad ibn al-Habib put one
foot up on the step and said, "Khawf," then his next foot
up and said, "Raja'." "Khawf! Raja'!" Shaykh Muhammad
ibn al-Habib, who at that point was one of the great 'ulama of Fes, who had no experience of Tasawwuf directly,
suddenly was confronted with another kind of man and
it had an effect on him. This man stayed with him and
Shaykh Muhammad ibn al-Habib never asked where he
had come from or why he was there, he accepted him as
his guest and asked him no questions, and the man stayed with him for almost two years.

In this time Shaykh Muhammad ibn al-Habib had seen
that this man was someone who never said anything
against anybody and if people spoke badly, liking to
gossip and attack people, he would leave the room. Also,
all the time he was doing Wird and making Ismul-
'Adham. Then one day he said, "I have a letter for you."

Shaykh Muhammad ibn al-Habib said, "I am not expecting any letters!" The man said, "It is for you!" He said, "Well then, it is from you. You read it." So he read out from his shaykh in Tinjdad giving Idhn to Shaykh Muhammad ibn al-Habib to take the Tariqa.

In all this the resonance which made him enter the Sufic path was the impact of this man climbing a stair where on every step he was poised between fear and hope. So this khawf is a reality for the mumin – that he has fear of Allah. "Do not fear them – fear Me if you are muminun." This is the beginning of the correct relation of ʿibada.

Now we look at Surat az-Zumar (39:36-37):

$$\text{أَلَيْسَ اللَّهُ بِكَافٍ عَبْدَهُ}$$

$$\text{وَيُخَوِّفُونَكَ بِالَّذِينَ مِن دُونِهِ وَمَن يُضْلِلِ}$$

$$\text{اللَّهُ فَمَا لَهُ مِنْ هَادٍ ۝ وَمَن يَهْدِ اللَّهُ فَمَا لَهُ مِن مُّضِلٍّ}$$

$$\text{أَلَيْسَ اللَّهُ بِعَزِيزٍ ذِي انتِقَامٍ ۝}$$

Is Allah not enough for His slave?
Yet they try to scare you with others apart from Him.
If Allah misguides someone, he has no guide
and if Allah guides someone, he cannot be misguided.
Is Allah not Almighty, Exactor of Revenge?

We are now understanding the 'Who' of Allah, how we can speak of Allah, Who is dealing with us because we cannot say that we are dealing with Him.

Allah is asking, "Is Allah not enough?" You must remember that we have all been educated with a materialist education. We have all received an education which believed that we had to master things and by mastering things it extended that we had to master people. The Deen of Islam does not accord with this, which is why in the present day you have such a chaos because people are trying to behave with that education and viewpoint as Muslims. This is why you have this horrible situation in Palestine and the horrible situation of all the Arab peoples for whom this is their language they use over breakfast.

They do not know, because they have taken on this world-view of the kuffar, and yet here the Revelation is saying: "Is Allah not enough for His slave?" This is a tremendous statement. Are you then looking for some other power to take you through the whole process of your life? Do you really think that there is some process that you can do that is going to support you when the Islamic position is that all you are called upon is not to do nothing, but to obey Allah? And if you obey Allah, He is enough for you. You do not need anything else. The things in turn will obey you.

"Is Allah not enough for you? Yet they try to scare you with others apart from Him" – that is coming out of the television set every day. That is what the news is – to make you feel that power lies elsewhere than with Allah, subhanahu wa ta'ala.

وَمَن يُضْلِلِ اللَّهُ فَمَا لَهُ مِنْ هَادٍ

40

If Allah misguides someone he has no guide.

The word for guide is Hadi. One of the Names of Allah is Al-Hadi so if you are not guided by the One who Guides then you are not going to be guided. There is not some other guidance that you will get that will take you through the process of life with success. "If Allah misguides someone, he has no guide and if Allah guides someone, he cannot be misguided." In other words the people who follow in this path of Allah, subhanahu wa ta'ala, they are safe, they are secure.

Then Allah says: "Is Allah not Almighty, Exactor of Revenge?" He is All-Powerful but he also takes revenge. So it is reminding you that this One you are being guided by is not going to let off those people who oppose you. They are not going to escape. This One who is All-Powerful, who is guiding the muminun, is also the One who will take a terrible revenge on those who do not obey Him. This also means that what you might call the 'foreign policy' of the Muslims has to be based on this. The transaction of the Muslims has to be based on this. This is part of the power of Allah, subhanahu wa ta'ala – that He does not let the enemy of Allah escape.

We come now to a very important thing which you have to remember because it is something that the Sufis lean very heavily on for the knowledge to give them strength and insight. It runs right through the Futuhat al-Makkiyya of Shaykh Ibn al-'Arabi where he talks about Allah, subhanahu wa ta'ala, as the Creator. Allah says in Surat az-Zumar (39:38):

وَلَئِن سَأَلْتَهُم مَّنْ
خَلَقَ ٱلسَّمَوَٰتِ وَٱلۡأَرۡضَ لَيَقُولُنَّ ٱللَّهُ

If you ask them,
'Who created the heavens and the earth?'
they will say, 'Allah'.

What Allah is telling us by this is that the kuffar are not necessarily atheists but that they have in fact limited Allah. The kuffar think they live in an already-created reality and then on this created reality they run wild and do what they like. This is not the truth of the matter.

In the rest of the ayat Allah, subhanahu wa ta'ala, shows them that that is not how it is. There is nothing in creation that is not in the process of action. Allah is One in His Names and His Attributes and His Essence, and He has created the things in a dynamic state. Therefore not only the human beings, the animals, the living organisms, but even the chemical foundation of the world, the mountains, what Ibn al-'Arabi called the 'gypsum foundation' of creation – all of these things are in motion. Anyone who has any doubt should look at what has been happening in Turkey and look at what has been happening in Iran. The mountains and valleys have been erupting, splitting, everything is in motion – there are gases coming out of the earth at every minute, the whole thing is alive.

The evolutionary lie is that there were these simple organisms which got more and more complex and then, poff! you have man, and that is the creational process. Then this man does what he wants, he makes up his rules, he makes up his ideas – the whole of the eighteenth century was men making up ideas about how they should live and what existence was – they invented the whole thing!

Allah is telling us that the kuffar will say that Allah created the heavens and the earth but that is not understanding because you cannot separate a man from his actions. Therefore the creation of man enclothes the fulfilment of the destiny of the man. That is part of His creation, it is part of the creativity, just as the creation of the birds, the animal kingdom involves the whole cycle of mating and reproduction. For instance, the whole cycle of hibernation of the bears – there is no such thing as a bear without hibernation, it is not possible. So creation goes through the seasons, it goes through life.

When the kuffar give this insufficient answer, Allah, subhanahu wa ta'ala, tells us to respond with this:

$$\text{قُلْ أَفَرَءَيْتُم مَّا تَدْعُونَ مِن دُونِ ٱللَّهِ إِنْ أَرَادَنِيَ ٱللَّهُ بِضُرٍّ هَلْ هُنَّ كَٰشِفَٰتُ ضُرِّهِ أَوْ أَرَادَنِي بِرَحْمَةٍ هَلْ هُنَّ مُمْسِكَٰتُ رَحْمَتِهِۦ}$$

Say: 'So what do you think?
If Allah desires harm for me,
can those you call upon besides Allah remove His harm?
Or if He desires mercy for me
can they withhold His mercy?'

In other words, all this dynamic process of life which the kuffar call history and which the sociologists call social relations and so on, is actually under the command of Allah, subhanahu wa ta'ala. When good comes it is from Allah, when trouble comes it is from Allah and they cannot control how Allah works with His creation, making it happen.

The position of wisdom is then given:

$$\text{قُلْ حَسْبِيَ اللَّهُ عَلَيْهِ يَتَوَكَّلُ الْمُتَوَكِّلُونَ} \; \textcircled{\tiny ٣٨}$$

Say: 'Allah is enough for me.
All those who truly trust put their trust in Him.'

Allah, subhanahu wa ta'ala, has set out that there is in the human race a body of people who have another orientation which by its nature, because it contains the wisdom about how existence works, has to triumph. But they can only triumph if they are in that circle of the muminun who are defined by 'ibada, and their visa, their passport is 'ibada.

Look at Surat al-Hadid (57:22):

$$\text{مَا أَصَابَ مِن مُّصِيبَةٍ فِي الْأَرْضِ وَلَا فِي أَنفُسِكُمْ إِلَّا فِي} $$
$$\text{كِتَابٍ مِّن قَبْلِ أَن نَّبْرَأَهَا إِنَّ ذَٰلِكَ عَلَى اللَّهِ يَسِيرٌ} \; \textcircled{\tiny ٢٢}$$

Nothing occurs, either in the earth or in yourselves,
without its being in a Book before We make it happen.
That is something easy for Allah.

This is the depths of the wisdom of Qur'an which is only to be found in Qur'an. Allah, subhanahu wa ta'ala, opens up all His treasures of His secrets to the muminun. "It is in a Book," means that it has already been stated, it has already been sent down. The history is told.

Sayyiduna 'Umar ibn al-Khattab, radiyallahu 'anhu, was with Rasul, sallallahu 'alayhi wa sallam, and he asked, "O Rasul! Are we on a matter that is just beginning or are we on a matter that is just finished?" Rasul, sallallahu 'alayhi wa sallam, said, "The Book is written and the ink is dry." 'Umar ibn al-Khattab then said, "If that is the case, what then is the use of my making an effort to do things if it is already determined what is going to happen?" Rasul, sallallahu 'alayhi wa sallam, said, "Every creature is on a pattern from Allah and he will do that which is the destined thing for him, and he cannot escape it." 'Umar ibn al-Khattab said, "Now I can go back to work." Look at the quality of those people. That did not stop him, he said that he was one of those people who would do the utmost to serve Allah and, "I will go back to work."

It was not an imprisoning thing or a crushing thing but a liberating thing. That is why the muminun make the du'a, "O Allah, give me an Iman that is lasting." You want the seal of the destiny to be secure so that you die in Islam, so that your path all the way through is dynamic. This is something easy for Allah. Then in the next ayat of Surat al-Hadid Allah says:

$$\text{لِّكَيْلَا تَأْسَوْا عَلَى مَا فَاتَكُمْ وَلَا تَفْرَحُوا بِمَا آتَاكُمْ}$$

That is so that you will not be grieved
about the things that pass you by
or exult about the things that come to you.

This is very significant because Allah defines for the mumin, like the question of 'Umar ibn al-Khattab, the condition in which he is left. These two opposites do not
anymore impinge on your heart. Once you understand
how things are, you will not be grieved about the things
that have passed you by. There is no such thing as having
missed something. That is it! That is the who-ness of
you. And you do not exult about the things that come to
you because they have come by the destiny and by the
same power of the One who has held other things back
from you. So you become unified in your understanding
of Tawhid.

Surat az-Zumar (39:62-64):

$$\text{اللَّهُ خَالِقُ كُلِّ شَيْءٍ وَهُوَ عَلَى كُلِّ شَيْءٍ وَكِيلٌ ۝}$$

Allah is the Creator of everything
and He is Guardian over everything.

Look at the uncompromising viewpoint that is offered
the Muslim, it is like standing on granite, it puts you on
firm foundations. You cannot be shaken because once
you grasp the Tawhid of Allah you are men of knowledge, you know how existence works. You must realise
that the kafirun do not know what is going on. They do
not understand the process. The Muslims who have

taken knowledge from the Book of Allah and from the Sunna of Rasul, sallallahu 'alayhi wa sallam, they know that Allah is the Creator of everything and He is the Guardian over everything. If He is the Guardian over everything, then He is the Guardian over you and you will move in a confidence that what you will do is that which will best secure your safety. This includes everything, including war. It is an understanding of security and safety that is inside the person.

This next thing is very important. Allah, subhanahu wa ta'ala, says:

$$\text{لَّهُۥ مَقَالِيدُ ٱلسَّمَٰوَٰتِ وَٱلۡأَرۡضِۗ وَٱلَّذِينَ كَفَرُواْ بِـَٔايَٰتِ ٱللَّهِ أُوْلَٰٓئِكَ هُمُ ٱلۡخَٰسِرُونَ} \circledcirc$$

The keys of the heaven and earth belong to Him.
It is those who reject Allah's Signs who are the losers.

He does not say that just the heavens and earth belong to Him, we have already established that, He also says the keys of the heavens and earth. That is the patterns, and the patterns of the heavens are all those things that bring to life all the living forms from the Unseen into the Seen. So the disappearance of the species is under Allah's law as well as the appearance of the strong mumin at the time the Muslims need it. All these things are because Allah has the keys and He, subhanahu wa ta'ala, unlocks events.

We may not like the events which are unlocked, but the ones who have this strong Tawhid can read events and know what to do. For example, Rasul, sallallahu 'alayhi wa sallam, said that there will come a time when the best property will be sheep and to hide and retire in the mountains. Alhamdulillah, we have not reached that point, but there is a point when that will be the thing the mumin knows to do. The keys to the heavens are with Allah and also the keys of the earth belong to Him. This means that He unlocks events just as He unlocks living forms. He unlocks the earth and makes this earth sterile and makes this earth fertile. He makes this earth shake and He brings down a city. All of this is in His power that the patterns of existence are in His hands.

Allah says: "Those who reject Allah's signs are the losers." Allah's signs are those manifestations in existence of His power. Everything which is happening in the world is to teach the mumin, even the things we do not like, even the situation today with our Ummah – there are signs and Allah is giving us indications. What He disapproves of and what He approves of have not changed, so we have to interpret them and there are those things which awaken in the Muslims this vibration which we call khawf, that you fear Allah. At the same time, when things become intolerable, Allah also has a guidance that He never puts on the mumin more than he can bear.

Finally Allah says:

$$\text{قُلْ أَفَغَيْرَ اللَّهِ تَأْمُرُونِّي أَعْبُدُ أَيُّهَا الْجَاهِلُونَ ۝}$$

Say: 'Do you order me
to worship something other than Allah,
you ignorant people?'

The ignorant people are all those we are dealing with in
the world today, the atheists and the people who have cor-
rupted former religions who are completely lost. They are
ignorant. Our strength lies in our knowledge Allah has
given us through the Qur'an and through the pattern of
what is pleasing behaviour to Allah, subhanahu wa ta'ala,
which is that of the Rasul, sallallahu 'alayhi wa sallam.

Now we look at Surat al-Ahzab (33:41-43):

$$
\text{يَٰٓأَيُّهَا ٱلَّذِينَ ءَامَنُوا ٱذْكُرُوا ٱللَّهَ ذِكْرًا كَثِيرًا ۝ وَسَبِّحُوهُ}
$$
$$
\text{بُكْرَةً وَأَصِيلًا ۝ هُوَ ٱلَّذِي يُصَلِّي عَلَيْكُمْ وَمَلَٰٓئِكَتُهُۥ لِيُخْرِجَكُم}
$$
$$
\text{مِّنَ ٱلظُّلُمَٰتِ إِلَى ٱلنُّورِ ۚ وَكَانَ بِٱلْمُؤْمِنِينَ رَحِيمًا ۝}
$$

You who have Iman! Remember Allah much,
and glorify Him in the morning and the evening.
It is He who calls down blessing on you,
as do His angels,
to bring you out of the darkness into the light.
He is Most Merciful to the muminun.

Allah gives a direct order how to keep in you this inner
fulcrum, this inner compass that is going to put you into
a knowledgeable state about the events which come in
your life. You will know how to deal with the different

things of existence because everything in existence is alive
– you are not wandering in a desert but living through a
situation where everything is alive and full of possibilities which Allah is offering you and giving you at every
moment. You will know how to discriminate – one of
the names of the Book is the Furqan – and you will
know from this wisdom how to react in every situation.

Allah, subhanahu wa ta'ala, says: "You who have Iman!"
and then He says that the way the whole thing is kept
alive is: "Remember Allah much." This is the famous
phrase which repeats in the Qur'an, 'dhikr kathiran' –
lots of dhikr. Allah is saying that this reality you are
living in is so tremendous that while you have been given
the pattern which is enough for you there is much more.
You can go on and on by degrees because Allah explains
in Qur'an that the muminun are raised up by degrees of
Divine knowledge which they receive from Allah.

One of the Bedouin came to Rasul, sallallahu 'alayhi wa
sallam, and said, "Is it true that I have to confirm that
Allah is One and Muhammad, sallallahu 'alayhi wa sallam,
is His Messenger?" He said, "Yes." Then he asked, "Is it
true I have to make Salat five times a day?" He said, "Yes."
"Is it true I have to fast every year?" He said, "Yes." "Is it
true I have to pay the Zakat?" He said, "Yes." "Is it true I
have to take the Hajj?" He said, "Yes." "Well that is all I
know, I am not doing anything else!" Rasul, sallallahu
'alayhi wa sallam, said, "Then you will have success."

Another time, a Bedouin said to him, "I do the five
prayers, I am not doing anything else. That's it!" Rasul,

sallallahu 'alayhi wa sallam, smiled and said, "Allah will give you the Garden. He will reward you." In other words, because of the mercy of Allah the minimum is enough. Yet among the muminun there is an elite body of people who are not content with this, they want more. They have read in the Qur'an that Allah raises people up by degrees and the highest degree is the people called the Muqarrabun, the people who draw near to Allah. Because He has not got place, Allah has explained: "Allah is nearer to you than your jugular vein," so it is a nearness which has no spatiality in it at all. This nearness is the condition of the 'Arifin and the salihun. This is the Qur'anic language for the Sufi. The Muqarrabun are the Sufis.

"Glorify Him in the morning and the evening" – that is in the Fajr and after the Isha. "It is He who calls down blessing on you, as do His angels, to bring you out of the darkness into the light." The interesting thing is that in another part of the Qur'an (Surat al-Ahzab, 33:56), Allah specifically says about the Rasul, sallallahu 'alayhi wa sallam:

$$\text{إِنَّ ٱللَّهَ وَمَلَٰٓئِكَتَهُۥ يُصَلُّونَ عَلَى ٱلنَّبِيِّ ۚ}$$
$$\text{يَٰٓأَيُّهَا ٱلَّذِينَ ءَامَنُوا۟ صَلُّوا۟ عَلَيْهِ وَسَلِّمُوا۟ تَسْلِيمًا ۝}$$

Allah and His angels
call down blessings on the Prophet.
You who have Iman! call down blessings on him
and ask for complete peace and safety for him.

But here it is more. One cannot make a mistake about this so we went to the great tafsir of Shaykh Ibn 'Ajiba who says that Allah says: "My Salat is a mercy on you, sallallahu 'alayhi wa sallam, and on your Ummah." Now, with overflowing love of Allah, subhanahu wa ta'ala, He makes the salat on Rasul, sallallahu 'alayhi wa sallam, and the angels on the whole Ummah of the Muslims. So we are a community overwhelmed by the protection and love and the blessing of Allah, subhanahu wa ta'ala. It is because of him we all get this direct, Divine covering and protection and blessing of Allah, subhanahu wa ta'ala.

Then Allah, subhanahu wa ta'ala, says: "He is the Most Merciful to the muminun." We are in a position of absolute security, absolute safety and we cannot go wrong as long as we remember that He is the Lord of the Universe, and the Lord of our destinies. I think we will stop there, but there is more!

HADRA

We ask Allah, subhanahu wa ta'ala, to cover us in His Rahma. We ask from Allah a great forgiveness beyond anything we could merit. We ask Allah, subhanahu wa ta'ala, to cover our wrong action. We ask Allah, subhanahu wa ta'ala, to strengthen us in our good action. We ask Allah, subhanahu wa ta'ala, to make us people of good actions. We ask Allah, subhanahu wa ta'ala, to raise us up to degree after degree of knowledge. We ask Allah, subhanahu wa ta'ala, in all the destiny to give us an Iman that lasts to the grave. We ask Allah, subhanahu wa ta'ala, to let us die among the salihun and in the best of company.

We ask Allah, subhanahu wa ta'ala, to give victory to the Muslims. We ask Allah, subhanahu wa ta'ala, to pardon the Arabs for their having abandoned the Deen of Islam. We ask Allah, subhanahu wa ta'ala, in His Mercy to bring them back to the Deen by the secrets of His Qur'an. We ask Allah, subhanahu wa ta'ala, to revive the Muslims in every land. We ask Allah, subhanahu wa ta'ala, to remove the false 'ulama from their places. We ask Allah, subhanahu wa ta'ala, to remove the thrones from their places. We ask Allah, subhanahu wa ta'ala, to place thrones of honour and thrones of 'ibada to rule the Muslims. We ask Allah, subhanahu wa ta'ala, to give us leaders to restore us to our full splendour. We ask Allah, subhanahu wa ta'ala, to let it happen during the lives of the people here assembled. We ask Allah, subhanahu wa ta'ala, to protect the children of the people here assembled and to give them a world in which the Deen is stronger than it has ever been.

We ask Allah, subhanahu wa ta'ala, to make the people of this Tariqa travel wherever they want in the world and to establish the Deen wherever they go. We ask Allah, subhanahu wa ta'ala, for benefits beyond anything we deserve. We ask Allah, subhanahu wa ta'ala, to be generous to us by His promise of generosity and to give us generosity on our fellow Muslims in order to merit such generosity from Allah. We ask Allah, subhanahu wa ta'ala, whose generosity cannot be compared to ours, to be merciful to us, to strengthen us and to give us the Sirat al-Mustaqim into a future with hope dominating our fear.

III

APRIL 10TH 2004

We started with the subject of the adab of the mumin in relation to his 'ibada and I am just going to continue. It is something that has an ongoing path and this is one bit of it. Also, inshallah, we are going to stop at a very, not confusing, but contradictory part, so that I will also have to introduce the subject for next week, because otherwise you will think that this is the whole story! We are now moving into a very serious, deep matter so I ask you to please try and sit still and concentrate. Fold your hands, or look at the Qur'an.

We are now going to look at the subject of Allah as the Creator and then His creation, His creatures. We are looking at Allah in His power as Creator. So we look at Surat al-Hadid (57:1-3 and 6):

بِسْمِ اللهِ الرَّحْمَنِ الرَّحِيمِ

سَبَّحَ لِلَّهِ مَا فِي السَّمَوَاتِ وَالْأَرْضِ وَهُوَ الْعَزِيزُ الْحَكِيمُ ۝ لَهُ مُلْكُ السَّمَوَاتِ وَالْأَرْضِ يُحْيِـۦ وَيُمِيتُ وَهُوَ عَلَى كُلِّ شَيْءٍ قَدِيرٌ ۝ هُوَ الْأَوَّلُ وَالْآخِرُ وَالظَّاهِرُ وَالْبَاطِنُ وَهُوَ بِكُلِّ شَيْءٍ عَلِيمٌ ۝

In the name of Allah, All-Merciful, Most Merciful
Everything in the heavens and the earth glorifies Allah.
He is the Almighty, the All-Wise.
The kingdom of the heavens and the earth belong to Him.
He gives life and causes to die.
He has power over all things.
He is the First and the Last,
the Outward and the Inward.
He has knowledge of all things.

Then the last ayat is:

يُولِجُ اللَّيْلَ فِي النَّهَارِ وَيُولِجُ النَّهَارَ فِي اللَّيْلِ وَهُوَ عَلِيمٌ بِذَاتِ الصُّدُورِ ۝

He makes night merge into day
and day merge into night.
He knows what the heart contains.

We are beginning to get an understanding in these ayats about Allah as the Creator. "Everything in the heavens and the earth glorifies Allah. He is the Almighty, the All-Wise." The first thing is that everything in the heavens and the earth glorifies Allah. This is an indication of something that the Sufis and the salihun have understood for hundreds of years, and which the scientists have belatedly discovered in the last hundred years – the things of the heavens and the earth are not static and dead. Everything is alive. Everything is in action. The atom is not a static thing but a whirling, speeding thing. Everything is in motion and this motion is the glorification of Allah, subhanahu wa ta'ala.

مَا فِى السَّمَوَٰتِ وَالْاَرْضِ

Everything in the heavens and the earth.

'Heavens' is samawati, which also means those things which are in the Unseen, which are going to come into the existent realm to glorify Allah. In other words, the forms that have not emerged into the created world are also glorifying Allah, subhanahu wa ta'ala.

لَهُ مُلْكُ السَّمَوَٰتِ وَالْاَرْضِ

The kingdom of the heavens and the earth,

– the kingdom of the unseen world and the visible world – belongs to Him.

يُحْيِ وَيُمِيتُ

He gives life and He causes to die.

Part of this nature of the created event is the giving of life and the making to die. What happens in the span of time, between birth and death, coming into existence and going out of existence – this is all under the power of Allah, subhanahu wa ta'ala. It is His Action that brings to life and also terminates it. This means also that the creation of the living forms is under the power of Allah in its totality.

You must remember that part of the essence of kufr is the idea that the creation is a static thing into which comes man with an intellect which is then free to behave in a certain way. The understanding of the Muslims is that Allah is the Creator of the creatures, and also this means that the human being's actions are part of his existence. You cannot separate a man from his actions. What a man does in that span of time is all under the command of Allah, subhanahu wa ta'ala.

وَهُوَ عَلَىٰ كُلِّ شَيْءٍ قَدِيرٌ

He has power over all things.

This means that He is the activator of them. Power is not some magical thing that intervenes with 'free radicals' doing what they want and suddenly some divine force pounces on them. Power over them is, by His power, to let them do that which they are going to do. This is very important for the Muslims to understand.

$$\text{هُوَ ٱلْأَوَّلُ وَٱلْآخِرُ وَٱلظَّاهِرُ وَٱلْبَاطِنُ ۖ وَهُوَ بِكُلِّ شَيْءٍ عَلِيمٌ ٣}$$

He is the First and the Last,
the Outward and the Inward.
He has knowledge of all things.

This is a very important ayat for the Sufis. It is an ayat which has openings, Fatiha, in it for the 'Arif. Moulay al-'Arabi ad-Darqawi, radiyallahu 'anhu, explains how he achieved his Tawhid with Allah: when he was in khalwa, he heard a voice declaring this ayat. He heard this and said, "I understand that He is the First and the Last, and I understand that He is the Inward, but I do not understand how He is the Outward." He was saying that in his correct upbringing as an 'alim, of course, that Allah is exalted above everything that could be associated with Him. The voice then said, "If He had meant anything else He would have said it." This confirmation that He was not only the Inward but that He was the Outward was what gave him his Tawhid and he passed out of the consciousness of this world.

At the minute we are looking at this aspect of exalting Allah over everything with which He can be associated and yet, at the heart of it, we have to come back to this element about the nature of what we can say about Allah, confirmed by what He tells us, that He is the First and the Last, the Outward and the Inward.

$$\text{يُولِجُ ٱلَّيْلَ فِي ٱلنَّهَارِ وَيُولِجُ ٱلنَّهَارَ فِي ٱلَّيْلِ}$$
$$\text{وَهُوَ عَلِيمٌ بِذَاتِ ٱلصُّدُورِ ٦}$$

He makes the night merge into day
and day merge into night.
He knows what the heart contains.

While we are getting an understanding of Allah being exalted above the creation and having power over the creation, we also discover that the One who is the Master of the cosmic events of night and day – which means the whole nature of the creation of the stars and the sun and the moon –

$$\text{وَهُوَ عَلِيمٌ بِذَاتِ الصُّدُورِ ۝}$$

He knows what the breasts contain.

Sudur in Arabic means 'breasts' but it is more correct to say 'hearts' because it is saying that Allah knows what is inside the human creature. Inside the human creature is the impulse to action, the force to move and make things happen, to do things. It is not an emotional thing about being angry or not, "He knows what is in the heart," and the heart moves by impulse. The word qalb, which means heart, is from the root 'qalaba' which means to turn over, to transform, to change. So the very central organ of man is itself in motion with this Divine commotion that has been set up in it.

So you will find that Allah being exalted above everything and the Creator of everything is put alongside His power to know what is in the breasts of man.

Now we will go to Surat Ya Sin (36:82). We have come

to the point where we have to look at the created things because we have to understand the nature of how Allah is with His creation, which is not a simple matter and yet it is not a complicated matter. It is simply that you must see it with the eye of understanding. One of the great Sufis of India said: "This matter will never be settled by logic." It is like when you tell someone something and they get it: "I've got it!" It is not a mental process but a 'seeing the whole point of something.' This is how you will understand the nature of Tawhid.

$$ \text{إِنَّمَآ أَمْرُهُۥٓ إِذَآ أَرَادَ شَيْـًٔا أَن يَقُولَ لَهُۥ كُن فَيَكُونُ} \textcircled{٨٢} $$

His command when He desires a thing
is just to say to it, 'Be!' and it is.

Here Allah plunges us right into the secret of His secrets. He unveils it for the muminun openly. There are no mysteries in Islam, what is unveiled is unveiled. What the heart is able to grasp is another matter.

Allah's command when He desires a thing is just to say to it, 'Be!' and it is. Kun fa yakun – it is almost like the grammar breaks down because the 'fa' is very fine usage. It is not 'and' or 'it follows that', rather it is like you could put 'Be' then a stroke, then 'it is' – Be/it is. You have to concentrate on this because it is very strange. When Allah wants a thing, He just says to it "Kun fa yakun," "Be!" and it is. If you look at it one way it does not make sense. I am not being discourteous to Allah, I am unlocking this so you see it. Astaghfirullah, if Allah said this to it and it was there, it would not make sense because if it is already there, how does He say to it to be there? If it is not there, how can He say to it, "Kun fa yakun?" We have to understand this because neither of the ordinary outside situations click with common sense.

When Allah's Command, the Amr, comes on His desire, His Irada – when He wills it, it means that the thing is already in His knowledge, so He orders it and it is in being. In this sense we can understand, by metaphor, that the creator of forms has an idea of a form and then he makes it happen. At the moment we will stick with this very crude metaphor because we are going to find out something even more devastating and overwhelming about how Allah deals with His creation, to do with something that is not 'exalted above' but intimately close.

Before the thing comes into the creation – and we cannot say 'it is in the mind of Allah' because we have no authority to say that – but it is in the knowledge of Allah, subhanahu wa ta'ala. The thing is in His know-ledge and when He is ready and when He wills it, it comes into being. So we have taken one step into an understanding of Tawhid.

Now we go to Surat Maryam (19:9). Now Allah, subhanahu wa ta'ala, opens the doors, reveals the secrets. He explains His way of dealing with existence openly. Remember that we are not dealing with ayats of hukm, we are dealing with ayats that explain about existence. We would have to take a different adab to the ayats that say what is forbidden and permitted. At the moment we are dealing with Allah being the Creator.

$$قَالَ كَذَٰلِكَ قَالَ رَبُّكَ هُوَ عَلَيَّ هَيِّنٌ$$
$$وَقَدْ خَلَقْتُكَ مِن قَبْلُ وَلَمْ تَكُ شَيْئًا ۝$$

He said, 'It will be so!
Your Lord says, "That is easy for me to do.
I created you before, when you were not anything."'

This is about the gift of a child. There are just two things in this ayat and first of all – although we will not go into the details of it – the slave is being told of a generous gift of life to a child from Allah on the parent. The first part of it is that the slave, because he is of the salihun and of the exalted knowers, when he is told how it will be, although it does not seem to be possible, he accepts it. It is that acceptance of Allah's dealing with his slave that allows Allah, subhanahu wa ta'ala, to inform the slave of a knowledge that he did not have until he heard this.

$$قَالَ رَبُّكَ هُوَ عَلَيَّ هَيِّنٌ$$

Your Lord says, 'That is easy for Me to do.'

'Lord' means the Rabb, Allah, in His capacity to create all the living forms and all the inter-connectedness of all the forms. This is Rububiyyat, which is from Rabb, and Rububiyyat involves not only the creation of the forms but also their connectedness, like all the levels of the forest from the tops of the trees down to the insects at the root of the tree. All these are interconnected just as the nations of men and the movements of men, and the vast migrations of men all come under Rububiyyat.

So this is the Lord saying that He will give this child, and then He says:

$$وَقَدْ خَلَقْتُكَ مِن قَبْلُ وَلَمْ تَكُ شَيْئًا ۝$$

I created you before, when you were not anything.

So He explains to the father the commentary on Kun fa yakun: "I created you before, when you were not anything." First of all you were not anything, the command came, "Kun!" and you were. Allah created you so that there was a 'you' to create. We find when we look elsewhere in Qur'an that in fact all the human creatures were called before Allah, subhanahu wa ta'ala, before the creation of the world and He said to them (7:172):

$$أَلَسْتُ بِرَبِّكُمْ$$

Am I not your Lord?

This is how Allah, subhanahu wa ta'ala, deals with the creation. It is a dynamic, ongoing event in the in-time. All the in-time is under His power, which is beyond time and is not associated with anything.

We go to Surat al-Mulk (67:13-14):

$$وَأَسِرُّواْ قَوْلَكُمْ أَوِ اجْهَرُواْ بِهِ إِنَّهُ عَلِيمٌ بِذَاتِ الصُّدُورِ ۝$$

Whether you keep your words secret or say them out loud,
He knows what the heart contains.

Again we get this reminder that He knows what the
breasts contain. This impulse of the human heart to go
this way or that way, to be secretive or open – all this, He
knows what the heart contains. This is about the absolute command that Allah, subhanahu wa ta'ala, has over
the slave.

$$\text{أَلَا يَعْلَمُ مَنْ خَلَقَ وَهُوَ اللَّطِيفُ الْخَبِيرُ}$$

Does He who created not then know?
He is the All-Pervading, the All-Aware.

He is the Creator so Allah, subhanahu wa ta'ala, says,
'How am I not to know since you are my creation?' This
is the dynamic relationship into which Allah, subhanahu
wa ta'ala, is putting his slaves. He is not only putting the
muminun into this position, He is putting the kuffar in
this position. He is keeping those who behave in one
way in this position, and those who behave in another
way in this position, which means that this Divine knowledge is present in every situation.

"Does He who created not then know?" You must not
think that Allah made the universe and the stars and the
constellations, and then life came into things – this is the
position of the kuffar. The position of the Muslim is that
alongside this enormous cosmic majesty of Allah's creation, subhanahu wa ta'ala, there is also the fact of His
intimate connection to His slave. The Names He gives

are Al-Latif and Al-Khabir, which Hajj 'Abdalhaqq Bewley has heroically called the All-Pervading and the All-Aware. He has also said that Latif has the meaning of graciousness and kindness and also of penetrating right through everything, pervasive but with infinite kindness and closeness. Khabir is total awareness that takes in everything all the time. This is how we must understand Allah, subhanahu wa ta'ala, all the time.

We go back to Surat Ya Sin (36:79) for a vital phrase:

$$ \text{وَهُوَ بِكُلِّ خَلْقٍ عَلِيمٌ ۝} $$

He has total knowledge of each created thing.

The One you worship when you say, "Allahu akbar," – the 'akbar' of your takbir is that He has total knowledge of each created thing. Total knowledge not only means the biological creature but everything that is in it, its history from the moment of it coming into the world until the moment of its death. Allah, subhanahu wa ta'ala, knew you at birth and was aware of you when you died. This is the knowledge Allah has when He says that He has total knowledge of each created thing.

To realise the majesty of Allah and also this reality of Divine Presence is to realise that it is also a knowledge that involves all the creatures from the beginning of time until the in-time comes to an end. It is one process, and this process is the knowledge of Allah, subhanahu wa ta'ala.

We are going to look at how the mutakallimun see this.

What we are faced with is that the creature is known to Allah in the Unseen and the 'Kun' brings the creature into the seen world, into the existent world. The mutakallimun call the forms in the knowledge of Allah before they are created, the 'known'. They are known by Allah, but the Sufis have a special term for them because they think it is very important to get this thing right, so the Sufis have invented a vocabulary based on the Qur'anic ayats. They call this 'al-'Ayan ath-thabita' which means 'source-forms', although it is difficult to translate. 'Al-'Ayan ath-thabita' is when Allah has the – I do not like to use the word – 'idea' because this is not correct, but He has the form in His knowledge before the 'kun' brings it into existence. The Sufis call it a source-form, a form from the Source.

At this stage of our understanding of Tawhid we have to make a complete division, otherwise we will go outside Tawhid. We make a division between the known – that is the 'ayn ath-thabita before it comes into creation, before the 'kun' – and the Knower, Allah, subhanahu wa ta'ala. The known has a form, limited, determined, individual-ised, specific. The Knower is free of limitation, free of determination and is not a form. The known subsists only in the knowledge of the Knower, it has no independent existence until the 'kun'. The Knower exists in Himself, totally independent, He is not dependent on anything. Surat al-Ikhlas:

بِسْمِ اللَّهِ الرَّحْمَنِ الرَّحِيمِ

قُلْ هُوَ اللَّهُ أَحَدٌ ۝ اللَّهُ الصَّمَدُ ۝ لَمْ يَلِدْ وَلَمْ يُولَدْ ۝ وَلَمْ يَكُن لَّهُ كُفُوًا أَحَدٌ ۝

In the name of Allah, All–Merciful, Most Merciful
"Say: 'He is Allah, Absolute Oneness,
Allah, the Everlasting Sustainer of all.
He has not given birth and was not born.
And no one is comparable to Him.'"

The known has no attribute but it has a capacity in its form to receive attributes. The Knower is the possessor of these Source Attributes. Allah, subhanahu wa ta'ala, has these Attributes: life, knowledge, will, power, hearing, sight and speech. So when He makes the order: "Kun! fa yakun," He gives a bit of life, a bit of knowledge, a bit of will, a bit of power, a bit of hearing, a bit of sight, a bit of speech – we call them the borrowed attributes because they are in–time, and Allah is outside time but He lets the form, when it comes into being, have a limited 'rental'. The human being has a rental on these capacities or attributes because he is designed in order to be able to receive them.

The known forms, before they come into existence, are passive, have no existence, no attributes and no activity. When the 'kun' comes they can then have these things from Allah, subhanahu wa ta'ala, because the Knower has activity, the Knower is active, He is the Actor. All the actions of the creatures come from the Actor. There is no action of the creatures but from the gift of Allah, subhanahu wa ta'ala, in the order of the 'Kun! fa yakun.' Power belongs absolutely to Allah and He gives these, like sprinkling water, onto the forms to bring them to life.

Thus we are able to say that the relation of the known to

the Knower, of the forms to the Creator of the forms is
otherness. The forms are other-than-Allah, they are ghayr,
they are masiwallah. Everything that is existent, in the
world, in the cosmos is other-than-Allah: we have two.
This may sound very strange but to arrive at Tawhid we
must posit a very powerful 'two' because otherwise we
are not going to get it right. We would end up like the
mushriks or the kuffar.

Let us look at Surat Al 'Imran (3:28 & 30). It is one
phrase which comes twice:

$$وَيُحَذِّرُكُمُ ٱللَّهُ نَفْسَهُ$$

Allah advises you to be afraid of Him.

Hajj 'Abdalhaqq has very wisely given a different aspect
of the word 'yuhadhirukum' in each of these two ayats.
In one ayat: "Allah advises you to be afraid of Him," and
in the other: "Allah advises you to beware of Him."
What this is, is that Allah says not to try to understand
the Essence. The Act of Allah you must understand, the
Attributes of Allah you must understand, but when we
come to the Essence from which these complex things
emerge – do not try. Be afraid. Beware, because you
cannot penetrate it.

Also, Rasul, sallallahu 'alayhi wa sallam, in a famous
hadith, because of these revelations, warned the muminun not to contemplate, in the language of the mutakallimun, the 'Dhat', the Essence of Allah, subhanahu wa
ta'ala. Imam al-Ghazali goes to great lengths very

beautifully trying to understand it by looking at all the processes of the Act. Dependent on the Act are the Attributes: without the capacity to move and so on, you cannot realise something, but when you go from the Act to the Attributes that make it happen you ask, "Where do the Attributes come from?" and you reach the Essence. Imam al-Ghazali tries very beautifully to see if he can get any further but he stops and says that you cannot go any further. That is as far as you can go.

So let us say, in the language of the mutakallimun and the 'ulama, that Allah is Khaliq, the Creator, and the creatures are makhluq. Allah is Rabb, and the creatures are marbub. Allah is Ilah, He is worshipped, and the creatures are maluh, worshippers. Allah is Maalik with a long 'a', He is Master, Controller of all the destinies, and the slaves are mamluk. The Sufis say very beautifully:

"The Haqq is Existence, the 'abd is non-existence. Transformation of Reality is not possible, so the Haqq is Haqq and the 'abd is 'abd." The Lord is the Lord and the slave is the slave.

This means that all these shayateen of the orientalists who say that the Sufis are pantheists and say that God is the creation, have not understood anything at all of what is being taught. People talk about 'Wahdat al-wujud' yet the term does not appear once in all the four hundred books of Ibn al-'Arabi. When they talk about that they imply that God IS the universe. But the slave is the slave and the Lord is the Lord. Shaykh Ibn al-'Arabi says, "There is no limit to slavehood. There is no line by which he can pass over from created to Creator. There is no way that the Creator in His vastness will allow that He should be slave. He has, by His wisdom, determined it this way, this is how He set up creation."

We now go to the famous and well-known ayat in Surat Fatir (35:15):

$$\text{يَٰٓأَيُّهَا ٱلنَّاسُ أَنتُمُ ٱلۡفُقَرَآءُ إِلَى ٱللَّهِ ۖ وَٱللَّهُ هُوَ ٱلۡغَنِيُّ ٱلۡحَمِيدُ ۝}$$

O Mankind, you are the poor, in need of Allah,
whereas Allah is the Rich-beyond-need,
the Praise-Worthy.

This is a statement of what I have just said. The creature is totally dependent and Allah is totally Independent. The position of the slave in need of Allah is that he is in need of Allah for his living, his knowing, his seeing, his hearing, his willing – for all these attributes he needs this gift of Allah which has been given because He has made a form that can receive these capacities during the in-time span that is destined for him. But he is totally dependent, and Allah is totally independent of that creature and of that creature's functioning with these attributes that He has allowed him in the in-time to touch upon.

At this point we have to say that the essence of Tawhid is based on this fundamental duality, that Allah is highly exalted above anything that can be associated with Him. This does not change, but we are going to enter into another zone of knowledge which Allah has opened to us in the Qur'an which involves the nearness of Allah, subhanahu wa ta'ala. The slave is not just looking up in terror and awe at the majesty of a distant Creator, he is also conscious that the One who is the Creator of the universe, of the stars, of the planets, of the sun and moon and the other creatures and the land that they are on, is this One Who is close to you.

I think we had better look at one more ayat, otherwise I would leave you with a position which is not actually the whole, proper position of the Muslims. We have to look at the 'ananiyya', the 'I'-ness of the creature in this position of 'abd, before this Almighty Creator – otherwise we would all go home depressed! We will put just one foot in the door of this subject.

Look at Surat al-Hadid (57:4). By the way, this refers to the creation in six days. We know from other ayats in the Qur'an that the six days are not literally six days. You have to remember something which many people forget – there were not 'days' until Allah placed the earth in orbit around the sun. Days only happen once the whole thing is already done. When, in another place, Allah says that a day with Allah is like fifty thousand years in the way you count – it is like a phase in the creation over a time-span that is beyond our knowledge. The people who want to attack the Qur'an with ignorance say, "Six days? We know better than that, we are scientists," but they do not know anything.

هُوَ ٱلَّذِى خَلَقَ ٱلسَّمَٰوَٰتِ وَٱلْأَرْضَ فِى سِتَّةِ أَيَّامٍ
ثُمَّ ٱسْتَوَىٰ عَلَى ٱلْعَرْشِ

It is He who created the heavens and the earth in six days, then established Himself firmly on the Throne.

By 'throne' He means the cosmic Throne of the might of the creation.

$$\text{يَعْلَمُ مَا يَلِجُ فِي الْأَرْضِ وَمَا يَخْرُجُ مِنْهَا}$$
$$\text{وَمَا يَنزِلُ مِنَ السَّمَاءِ وَمَا يَعْرُجُ فِيهَا}$$

He knows what goes into the earth
and what comes out of it,
what comes down from heaven
and what goes up into it.

He knows the whole creational process. Then, having made this declaration about the majesty of Allah, He says:

$$\text{وَهُوَ مَعَكُمْ أَيْنَ مَا كُنتُمْ وَاللَّهُ بِمَا تَعْمَلُونَ بَصِيرٌ ۝}$$

He is with you wherever you are –
Allah sees what you do.

Allah has what you might call an 'intimate' connection, but it is not a connection because one cannot use the word connection. He has an intimate presence with the slave. He is with you wherever you are and Allah sees what you do.

The one who has understood this has a different experience of existence. Allah, subhanahu wa ta'ala, says in Surat al-Kahf (18:24):

وَاذْكُر رَّبَّكَ إِذَا نَسِيتَ

Remember your Lord when you forget.

So it is not someone forgetting the 'Asr prayer, or just being distracted by something in life, by things in the dunya, it is this. When you forget that He is with you wherever you are, and Allah sees what you do – when you forget that, that is what you have to remember. How He is with His creation – this is what you have to remember.

Surat al-Asr (103:2):

إِنَّ ٱلإِنسَـٰنَ لَفِى خُسْرٍ ۝

Truly man is in loss.

What is the loss of man? It is this. What does he forget? He forgets that Allah is with you wherever you are and Allah sees what you do. To finish, we remember the great Sufi of the East, Sahl at-Tustari, radiyallahu 'anhu, when he took as his wird, the Wird as-Sahl:

الله معي الله ناظر إلي الله شاهد علي

Allah is with me, Allah sees me,
Allah is the Witness of my acts.

That was the path to high Tawhid and to quick access to fana fillah and being obliterated in the Presence of Allah.

IV

APRIL 17TH 2004

What we have been doing is taking steps, and each gathering we have had is another step. This is just an instalment and there is, as it were, another chapter where we will join things that we have separated.

Hajj 'Abdalhaqq said something earlier which I was very pleased with in his understanding of what I had been saying last week. He said, "The wahhabis start with 'One', with a Tawhid which they declare, and they end up with two. What you are saying is that you start with two and you end up with One." So we are going towards a complete understanding of Tawhid but we have to go in stages because we are talking about the Tawhid of the people of the Tariqa, the people who are on the path to 'Ilm al-laduni, to direct knowledge of Allah, subhanahu wa ta'ala. You cannot afford to get it wrong.

All the foundations become the instruments and technical apparatus by which the Sufis reach their goal. They do not walk naked on their path. It is like the tawaf – before Rasul, sallallahu 'alayhi wa sallam, the people used to go naked around the Ka'aba. When Rasul came, sallallahu 'alayhi wa sallam, he did not abolish the tawaf but he had people clothed and gave them honour by being dressed, and he allowed the institution of tawaf to continue. Islam is not culture, Islam purifies culture. In the same way, for this knowledge that we want, you have to be clothed in this taqwa and this birr, this path of right action in order to arrive at the robe of honour which is Ma'rifatullah.

If we can continue the story as it were, we finished on the next stage of this matter which was in Surat al-Hadid (57:4). "It is He Who created the heavens and the earth in six days, then established Himself firmly on the Throne." We will look at it again because it gives us continuity: "It is He Who created the heavens and the earth in six days," and remember of course that the six days are not a literal thing but are part of this vision of the creation of the world where another ayat in the Qur'an refers to a day being an enormous length of time. "It is He Who created the heavens and the earth in six days, then established Himself firmly on the Throne" – then the whole cosmic reality came into being.

هُوَ ٱلَّذِى خَلَقَ ٱلسَّمَوَٰتِ وَٱلۡأَرۡضَ فِى سِتَّةِ أَيَّامٍ ثُمَّ ٱسۡتَوَىٰ عَلَى
ٱلۡعَرۡشِۚ يَعۡلَمُ مَا يَلِجُ فِى ٱلۡأَرۡضِ وَمَا يَخۡرُجُ مِنۡهَا وَمَا يَنزِلُ مِنَ ٱلسَّمَآءِ
وَمَا يَعۡرُجُ فِيهَاۖ وَهُوَ مَعَكُمۡ أَيۡنَ مَا كُنتُمۡۚ وَٱللَّهُ بِمَا تَعۡمَلُونَ بَصِيرٌ ۝

It is He Who created the heavens
and the earth in six days,
then established Himself firmly on the Throne.
He knows what goes into the earth
and what comes out of it,
what comes down from heaven and what goes up into it.
He is with you wherever you are –
Allah sees what you do."

I shall just remind you that the significance of us looking
at this ayat is that two knowledges which Allah reveals
about Himself are put together. This is this next step that
we are taking.

At the beginning of the ayat Allah, subhanahu wa ta'ala,
declares Himself the One Who created the whole cosmic reality but the next stage is: "He knows what goes
into the earth and what comes out of it, what comes
down from heaven and what goes up into it." Therefore
He also has an on-going knowledge. In the continual
nature of existence Allah, subhanahu wa ta'ala, knows
everything that is happening. It is not the primitive idea
of a divinity that makes everything happen and then He
has done His job, astaghfirullah. Allah is explaining that
His knowledge also contains all the process of life for

which, in another context, from the Qur'an, we take the term 'Rububiyya' from the word 'Rabb.'

Rububiyya is the Divine control over all the inter-related aspects of existence – how the chemicals come together to produce other chemicals, how the elements interact with each other, how in the whole life of the forest from the tops of the trees to the creatures at the foot of the trees, each creature has a capacity to eat another creature so that it can live – all these things are interconnected and inter-related by this Rububiyya.

Now we come to the last part which is what is important to us.

وَهُوَ مَعَكُمْ أَيْنَ مَا كُنتُمْ وَاللَّهُ بِمَا تَعْمَلُونَ بَصِيرٌ ﴿٤﴾

He is with you wherever you are –
Allah sees what you do.

This is a new knowledge that Allah is giving us. It has two things: it has 'ayna ma' which indicates place. So Allah knows the place where it is happening, and 'kuntum', 'you are', which indicates time, Allah sees the time and the place of any given human situation.

Allah sees what you do. As the mufassirin observe, Allah, subhanahu wa ta'ala, does not use the word 'know' which He could say if the meaning were about this earlier stage, but 'He is with you wherever you go' is Presence, and Allah sees what you do. 'Sees' from Basir, is the verb of eye-witnessing, and to witness you must be present.

$$وَاللَّهُ بِمَا تَعۡمَلُونَ بَصِيرٌ ۝$$

Allah sees what you do.

Basir is eye-witnessing. Therefore from this we have a
knowledge that Allah witnesses us, this is a seeing.

Now we go to Surat an-Nisa' (4:108):

$$يَسۡتَخۡفُونَ مِنَ ٱلنَّاسِ وَلَا يَسۡتَخۡفُونَ مِنَ ٱللَّهِ وَهُوَ
مَعَهُمۡ إِذۡ يُبَيِّتُونَ مَا لَا يَرۡضَىٰ مِنَ ٱلۡقَوۡلِ
وَكَانَ ٱللَّهُ بِمَا يَعۡمَلُونَ مُحِيطًا ۝$$

They try to conceal themselves from people,
but they cannot conceal themselves from Allah.
He is with them when they spend the night
saying things which are not pleasing to Him.
Allah encompasses everything they do.

People talk about the Qur'an as Revelation and you have
to understand that it IS a revelation! The Revelation is
not the descent of the Qur'an, it is that Allah reveals
secrets of Himself that have not been known until then.
He is telling us openly – it is a Qur'an al-Mubin, it is a
clear message. The Revelation is that Allah shows all His
secrets that He wants the human creatures to have, and
He gives it to them in this Book.

Here He says that people try to conceal themselves from
people, in other words these people are already in a

process of hiding themselves. But the Revelation says: "They cannot conceal themselves from Allah." In other words you can hide yourself from people but you cannot hide from Allah. This is a statement of how it is. This knowledge changes the one who has it. The one who knows this is not the same as the one who does not know. The ones who do not know try to conceal themselves from people. This is what kufr is – they cover over what is going on but they cannot be kafir with Allah, they are trying, but they cannot do it because Allah knows what is happening.

Then Allah says:

$$وَهُوَ مَعَهُمْ إِذْ يُبَيِّتُونَ مَا لَا يَرْضَىٰ مِنَ الْقَوْلِ$$

He is with them when they spend the night saying things which are not pleasing to Him.

Do you not see the reality of this? People are actually involved in the business of scheming against Allah, subhanahu wa ta'ala, against what is pleasing to Allah. So they are doing it as if they were in clandestine plotting against Allah. Allah says: "He is with them," and 'with them' is Presence.

$$وَكَانَ اللَّهُ بِمَا يَعْمَلُونَ مُحِيطًا ۝$$

Allah encompasses everything they do.

It is not something psychic or magical, but a Presence which encompasses the whole event of what they are doing. Apply this to how we get the news today. You get the news about Iraq and the news about Afghanistan and it is all presented to us by kuffar who are trying to conceal themselves from people, who are spending the night saying things that are not pleasing to Allah, but He says: "Allah encompasses everything they do." We have to see it in the light of Allah's complete command of the situation, He knows exactly what is happening. What He tells us is that He is with them, and that is Presence.

You have to understand that over this last century there has been a whole false teaching of Islam, a Tawhid that does not take into account these ayats that we are looking at, as if they did not exist. They have made a Tawhid by what Ibn al-'Arabi says, "They have had Tanzih but they have not had Tashbih." They have had exaltation of Allah above what is associated with Him without also understanding this extraordinary reality that Allah has openly declared in His Book about His Presence.

Rasul, sallallahu 'alayhi wa sallam, said in a well-known hadith, the meaning of which is: "None of you while making Salat should spit in front of himself as Allah, the Majestic, is before him." From this, the great collector of Sira, Asqalani, said, "This hadith refutes the claim of one who confines Allah to the 'Arsh alone. This establishes omnipresence in every place." This is very important because we are now getting a comprehension of Tawhid which allows us to say that, as we have already established, nothing can be associated with Him, He is not dependent on anything, He is not contained in any form, and at the same time here we have this amazing revelation of His Presence in events.

Let us look at Surat al-Waqi'a (56:83-87). What we are finding is that each one of these ayats is giving another dimension of this Presence of Allah, this witnessing of Allah, this seeing of Allah of the human actions. Now this nature of the Presence of Allah, subhanahu wa ta'ala, gets more intimate, more intense.

فَلَوْلَآ إِذَا بَلَغَتِ الْحُلْقُومَ ۞ وَأَنتُمْ حِينَئِذٍ
نَنظُرُونَ ۞ وَنَحْنُ أَقْرَبُ إِلَيْهِ مِنكُمْ وَلَكِن لَّا تُبْصِرُونَ ۞
فَلَوْلَآ إِن كُنتُمْ غَيْرَ مَدِينِينَ ۞ تَرْجِعُونَهَآ إِن كُنتُمْ صَدِقِينَ ۞

Why then, when death reaches his throat
and you are at that moment looking on –
and We are nearer him than you, but you cannot see –
why then, if you are not subject to Our command,
do you not send it back if you are telling the truth?

Allah is nearer the dying man than the man that is at his deathbed, but you cannot see. This is the most intense moment – a human being at the death of another human being, and at that moment the one who is watching the dying man does not understand that the nearness of Allah, subhanahu wa ta'ala, is nearer than his presence next to the dying man, and he cannot see. You are always on the edge of a Divine Presence, like that moment, for that moment is true at every moment.

"Why then, if you are not subject to Our judgment," to how We have decreed it to be – 'if you are telling the truth' – how the kafir sees it – 'why do you not send back this command of death, this destiny of death?' Allah has destined him to die. It is as if Allah were saying: 'If you,' the kafir, 'have this position that you claim then why do you not send back the order: 'Do not die!'' In other words you are denying the reality of the event of death thus denying the Presence of Allah, subhanahu wa ta'ala, in the act of death. This is the point that you have to understand. This knowledge of the Presence of Allah changes the experience of the one who knows it.

We go to Surat Qaf (50:16). Again, we will find two things coming together in this ayat.

وَلَقَدْ خَلَقْنَا الْإِنسَـٰنَ وَنَعْلَمُ مَا تُوَسْوِسُ بِهِۦ نَفْسُهُۥ وَنَحْنُ أَقْرَبُ إِلَيْهِ مِنْ حَبْلِ الْوَرِيدِ ۝

We created man and We know
what his own self whispers to him.
We are nearer to him than his jugular vein.

Look how Allah is unveiling His secrets to the people. Allah says, "We created man," and we have already understood that Allah has connected together this enormous physical creation and organisation of existence. Even the kuffar, as Allah says in Surat az-Zumar (39:38):

وَلَئِن سَأَلْتَهُم مَّنْ خَلَقَ السَّمَـٰوَٰتِ وَالْأَرْضَ لَيَقُولُنَّ اللَّهُ

If you ask them,
'Who created the heavens and the earth?'
they will say, 'Allah'.

What they do not see is (Surat Qaf, 50:16):

وَ

"Wa."

Every word in the Qur'an has meaning, every word is important.

لَقَدْ خَلَقْنَا ٱلْإِنسَـٰنَ

We created man

– it is not even 'created' but 'constructed', 'We constructed man, We put all the bits together that make up man,' and then comes, 'And'. You must think of creation in terms of the child in the womb. It structurally comes bit, by bit, by bit. The first organ to appear is the heart, then the other organs begin to form and come together bit by bit. This is what the 'khalaqna' is, it is almost 'constructed' in modern understanding.

So: "We constructed man," and the next bit is: "And we know what his own self whispers to him." The self's whisper is like a silent voice because it is inside the creature. Allah is saying that the One Who created this enormous cosmic event also knows what the self is saying to itself, what you are saying to yourself. So Allah is with you. You are accompanied by a Presence of Lordship – all the time. This is Tawhid! Now you are beginning to see what the true nature of Tawhid is.

Allah, subhanahu wa ta'ala, goes one step further to make the mind stop. He says:

$$\text{وَنَحْنُ أَقْرَبُ إِلَيْهِ مِنْ حَبْلِ الْوَرِيدِ ﴿١٦﴾}$$

We are nearer to him than his jugular vein.

He uses the word 'aqrab' for 'nearer' and Al-Qarib is a name of Allah, subhanahu wa ta'ala. Allah has Nearness. "We are nearer to him than his jugular vein." The jugular vein is what gives you life. If you cut the jugular vein you cut the life off. "We are nearer," and the Sufis find that the 'We' is often used with direct reference to the Essence, and what we are dealing with here is the Essence because there cannot be Attributes without Essence.

If Allah sees, if Allah hears, it means also that His Essence is there because He is not also divisible, He cannot be divided. Therefore again, this is a complete contradiction of the false teaching of Tawhid that has been spread among the Muslims over the last century which is why we are in the terrible situation that we are in now, and it is only this knowledge which you have, which you will take and teach, which will establish the true Qur'anic teaching, which is the might and power of Allah, subhanahu wa ta'ala, which means He is completely present in all our actions. In that sense, as slaves of Allah, we also know what He wants. This is how we will be able to change things because we have a knowledge that can only come through the people who have Iman, who have trust in Allah, subhanahu wa ta'ala.

Now we go to Surat al-Baqara which is filled with things of this nature. Surat al-Baqara (2:186):

$$\text{وَإِذَا سَأَلَكَ عِبَادِے عَنِّى فَإِنِّى قَرِيبٌ}$$

If My slaves ask you about Me, I am near.

Again there is this name of Allah – 'I am Near.' Mu'awiya ibn Ja'ad said, "Once a bedouin asked Rasul, sallallahu 'alayhi wa sallam, whether Allah was near to him so that he could talk intimately to Allah, or whether Allah was far so that he should shout." Rasul, sallallahu 'alayhi wa sallam, remained silent for a while then this ayat was revealed. This was the answer to the question of the bedouin.

$$\text{اجِيبُ دَعْوَةَ الدَّاعِ ـَ إِذَا دَعَانِ}$$

I answer the call of the caller when he calls on me.

Now we have been given another bit of the secret. This nearness of Allah is not a passive thing, it is dynamic and active. "I answer the call of the caller when he calls on Me." It is beautiful. The one who calls on Him, Allah calls on him. This is the true relationship of the slave with his Lord, a merciful Lord. It is an indication of the mercy of Allah, subhanahu wa ta'ala.

IV

$$\text{ٱجِيبُ دَعْوَةَ ٱلدَّاعِ ءَ إِذَا دَعَانِ}$$

I answer the call of the caller when he calls on Me,

– meaning that the one who calls on Him, He calls on them – so Allah calls, not His slave.

Then from this there is a conclusion:

$$\text{فَلْيَسْتَجِيبُواْ لِي وَلْيُؤْمِنُواْ بِي لَعَلَّهُمْ يَرْشُدُونَ ۝}$$

They should therefore respond to Me and believe in Me
so that hopefully they will be rightly guided.

In other words, once this knowledge clicks into place – and it is more than knowledge, it is an awareness of how things are – it follows that the person should respond to Allah. "They should therefore respond to Me and believe in Me," so you believe in Him, and you trust in Him because He is the Answerer. I cannot say it is a relationship because there is no relationship with Allah, but this possible reality comes into place through the knowledge that this is how things are. The calling makes the Iman.

Surat al-A'raf (7:7). This is another step in our understanding of this situation.

$$\text{فَلَنَقُصَّنَّ عَلَيْهِم بِعِلْمٍ وَمَا كُنَّا غَآئِبِينَ ۝}$$

We will tell them about it with knowledge.
We are never absent.

This is not a state that comes and goes, but it is constant. This is a knowledge which underlies all understanding of visible reality, which must be understood: Allah sees you, Allah hears you and He is never absent.

Abu Musa al-Ash'ari said that once, travelling with Rasul, sallallahu 'alayhi wa sallam, a companion started to shout takbir, and Rasul, sallallahu 'alayhi wa sallam, said, "O people, do not strain yourselves. You are not calling on One Who is blind or deaf. You are calling on the One Who is listening to you, seeing you and is with you. The One you are calling on is nearer to you than the neck of your camel." This is Rasul, sallallahu 'alayhi wa sallam, teaching Tawhid to the Sahaba – and denied for a hundred years by these shaytans from Arabistan. We have seen from these ayats that Allah sees what is happening and He hears the one who calls. You are calling on the One Who is listening to you, seeing you and is with you. The One you are calling on is nearer to you than the neck of your camels.

We now connect "We are never absent" to Surat an-Nisa' (4:126):

$$\text{وَلِلَّهِ مَا فِي السَّمَوَاتِ وَمَا فِي الْأَرْضِ}$$
$$\text{وَكَانَ اللَّهُ بِكُلِّ شَيْءٍ مُحِيطًا ﴿١٢٦﴾}$$

What is in the heavens
and in the earth belongs to Allah.
Allah encompasses all things.

IV

– which is the completion of what we saw in that last ayat. Allah possesses the whole situation and Allah encompasses all things. Not only is He never absent, but He encompasses everything. Surat al-An'am (6:103):

$$لَّا تُدْرِكُهُ الْأَبْصَـٰرُ وَهُوَ يُدْرِكُ الْأَبْصَـٰرَ$$

Eyesight cannot perceive Him
but He perceives eyesight.

Allah, subhanahu wa ta'ala, is constantly challenging the kuffar with the question: "On what grounds do you deny the Unseen, and given that you deny the Unseen how are you able to deny that you will be brought from your graves and held to account for your actions?" Allah, subhanahu wa ta'ala, says in Surat Fussilat (41:54):

$$أَلَا إِنَّهُمْ فِي مِرْيَةٍ مِّن لِّقَاءِ رَبِّهِمْ
أَلَا إِنَّهُ بِكُلِّ شَيْءٍ مُّحِيطٌ ۝$$

What! Are they in doubt
about the meeting with their Lord?
What! Does He not encompass all things?

It is like Allah has set up a contract with the human being and Allah, subhanahu wa ta'ala, is saying, "Do not deny it. How are you able to deny it?"

Allah says: "What! Are they in doubt about the meeting with their Lord?" He uses the word 'Rabb' which means 'Lord' in His aspect as the Ruler over all the created

89

creatures. "What! Are they in doubt about the meeting with their Lord?" Qur'an is insisting that this cannot be avoided, it cannot be doubted and if it is doubted then you are in ignorance because this meeting with the Lord, the encounter which happens after death is an inevitable and inescapable part of understanding the nature of the One Who has created the whole universe, Who is speaking through Rasul, sallallahu 'alayhi wa sallam, in the Revelation of Qur'an.

Surat at-Talaq (65:12):

$$\text{اللّٰهُ الَّذِي خَلَقَ سَبْعَ سَمٰوٰتٍ وَمِنَ الْأَرْضِ مِثْلَهُنَّ}$$
$$\text{يَتَنَزَّلُ الْأَمْرُ بَيْنَهُنَّ لِتَعْلَمُوا أَنَّ اللّٰهَ عَلٰى كُلِّ شَيْءٍ قَدِيرٌ}$$
$$\text{وَأَنَّ اللّٰهَ قَدْ أَحَاطَ بِكُلِّ شَيْءٍ عِلْمًا ۝}$$

It is Allah Who created the seven heavens
and of the earth the same number,
the Command descending down through all of them
so that you might know
that Allah has power over all things,
and that Allah encompasses all things in His
knowledge.

Allah, subhanahu wa ta'ala, is talking about His power as Creator not just of this earth but of the whole universe, the seven heavens and the seven realms of earth. Then He uses the word 'Amr' which is from the 'Kun!' – the Command of the creation of the cosmos descends through all the heavens and all the earth. This Amr goes

IV

to the furthest stars, to the furthest galaxies and constellations, "So that you might know that Allah has power over all things."

The Command has come through all the creation – in other words, part of the Command is that you are there on the earth to receive the message of Allah, subhanahu wa ta'ala, and know that He is the Creator of it, and that Allah encompasses all things in His knowledge.

Allah encompasses all things in His knowledge. He has made the whole cosmic event in His knowledge, but in the continuum He has created the time of the cosmos and knows it at every instant from its beginning, in its present, until its fulfilment. Remember the famous question of Sayyiduna 'Umar ibn al-Khattab, radiyallahu 'anhu, to Rasul, sallallahu 'alayhi wa sallam: "Are we on a matter that is finished or are we on a matter that is just beginning?" Rasul, sallallahu 'alayhi wa sallam, said, "The page is written and the ink is dry." "Allah encompasses all things in His knowledge" could not be true if He did not have a knowledge of everything to the Yawm al-Qiyama.

Remember also that time as we understand it stops with the creation. Again we come to the limits of thinking because it is in the nature of the Creator to create time. Rasul, sallallahu 'alayhi wa sallam, said, "Do not curse time because Allah is Time." There are two words for 'time', there is 'zaman' and 'dahr'. This means that Allah is the Creator of the instantaneousness of events, not just the measured distance of time. The measured distance of time will come to an end with the destruction of the world, but the moment in which the Command takes place is from Allah.

We now go back to Surat al-Baqara (2:115), and we are going deeper into this unveiling of Tawhid by Allah, subhanahu wa ta'ala.

$$وَلِلَّهِ الْمَشْرِقُ وَالْمَغْرِبُ$$
$$فَأَيْنَمَا تُوَلُّوا فَثَمَّ وَجْهُ اللَّهِ$$
$$إِنَّ اللَّهَ وَاسِعٌ عَلِيمٌ ۝$$

Both East and West belong to Allah,
so wherever you turn, the Face of Allah is there.
Allah is All-Encompassing, All-Knowing.

Let us look again at the Arabic:

$$وَلِلَّهِ الْمَشْرِقُ وَالْمَغْرِبُ$$

Both East and West belong to Allah,

– so the directions belong to Allah.

$$فَأَيْنَمَا تُوَلُّوا فَثَمَّ$$

"Fa thamma" – meaning, "right there –" and what comes immediately after that?

$$وَجْهُ اللَّهِ$$

"Wajhullah". Face of Allah. Do you see that there is no grammar, it is the Revelation of Allah, subhanahu wa ta'ala? There is no gap, there is no space in it, there is nothing added. "Wherever you turn – Face of Allah."

Knowledge is in making a distinction about this. This truth is so deep and so profound. There was once a famous majdhoub and they went into the mosque and he was prostrating here, there and everywhere and they said, "What do you think you are doing?" He said,

$$\text{فَأَيْنَمَا تُوَلُّوا فَثَمَّ وَجْهُ اللَّهِ}$$

"Wherever you turn, the Face of Allah is there." He was mad in love with Allah, going around in circles because, "There is the Wajh of Allah."

Look at the two aspects of this. If you go back into the Qur'an, Allah, subhanahu wa ta'ala, speaks with this intimacy and love and concern for Rasul, sallallahu 'alayhi wa sallam, and says to him in Surat al-Baqara (2:144):

$$\text{قَدْ بَرَىٰ نَقَلُّبَ وَجْهِكَ فِي السَّمَاءِ فَلَنُوَلِّيَنَّكَ قِبْلَةً تَرْضَىٰهَا فَوَلِّ وَجْهَكَ شَطْرَ الْمَسْجِدِ الْحَرَامِ}$$

We have seen you looking up into heaven,
turning this way and that,
so We will turn you towards a direction
which will please you.
Turn your face, therefore, towards the Masjid al-Haram.

Take the qibla of Makkah. So the Muslim takes a qibla and he takes it because that is Shari'ah. Shari'ah is that you take a direction. We cannot ask 'Why?' of Allah but I am trying to explain how the meaning of the taking the qibla of Makkah is the event of setting Islam above and abrogating all other religions. Otherwise he would have been permitted to make qibla of Jerusalem. It means the end of Jerusalem. It is the Deen of the qibla and Allah, subhanahu wa ta'ala, has given the muminun the qibla of Makkah. That is why Ibn Taymiyya quite rightly says, "There is no rite of 'ibada connected to Al-Aqsa." None. It is not in the Deen. It has a place for us of love and respect because of the Mi'raj, but the Deen involves the rites of Makkah.

You are then holding in your understanding two truths. One can only be understood in someone drunk and intoxicated with love of Allah, who is then outside the Shari'ah. If a man is mad and commits a crime he is not punished, he is locked up as insane. But the people have to obey the Law and the Law is that they take a qibla, which is ignorance unless you know that you take the qibla in slavehood, in your 'ubudiyya to Allah, subhana-hu wa ta'ala, because Rasul, sallallahu 'alayhi wa sallam, has been given the Revelation that that is how Allah wants us to make worship of Him. We do it, but we also know the Face of Allah is wherever you turn.

The Wajh of Allah, according both to the mutakallimun and the Sufis, is a way of saying the Essence of Allah. The Face of Allah is the Essence of Allah. The face of the person embodies, as it were, the person. Wherever you

turn, it means that the Essence of Allah is present. This
is also a denial of those who have set Allah on the Throne
and say that He has no presence on earth. It also gives a
lie to the ones who say, because of certain ayats in the
Qur'an, that Allah has limbs and is a person. Ibn Batutta's famous observation was that he heard Ibn Taymiyya
say, astaghfirullah, "Allah descends from His Throne as I
descend from this mimbar," which is of course a horrific
statement as far as we are concerned.

We now go to Surat al-Qasas (28:88) which we connect
to the previous ayat.

وَلَا تَدْعُ مَعَ اللَّهِ إِلَهًا آخَرَ لَا إِلَهَ إِلَّا هُوَ
كُلُّ شَيْءٍ هَالِكٌ إِلَّا وَجْهَهُ لَهُ الْحُكْمُ وَإِلَيْهِ تُرْجَعُونَ ۝

Do not call on any other god along with Allah.
There is no god but Him.
All things are passing except His Face.
Judgment belongs to Him. You will be returned to Him.

Here you have it. This is the dividing point. When
people say to you, "Dialogue with other faiths," there is
NO other faith, because they do not know this. This is
not to be debated or discussed, this is to be obeyed. This
is a knowledge only the Muslims have and if people want
knowledge they must come into the qasr, the fortress of
the Deen.

"Do not call on any other god along with Allah. There
is no god but Him. All things are passing except His

Face. Judgment belongs to Him. You will be returned to Him." Here is the complete contract.

$$\text{كُلُّ شَيْءٍ هَالِكٌ إِلَّا وَجْهَهُ}$$

All things are passing except His Face.

Everything that is in-time is passing, time is passing, all things are passing. This Divine Reality is before, during and after the 'all things' which are passing.

The Face of Allah is present, the Command – the 'Kun' is given, the things come into existence and by their coming into existence things move into an in-time sphere. From their beginning they are disintegrating and they pass. Everything passes except His Face, and when it is all gone – Wajh of Allah. The whole in-time movement of things comes to an end – Face of Allah. So Allah dominates and is the Reality in place and in time. Place is under His Command and under His Presence, and time is under His Command and under His Presence. This connects to another knowledge which is that judgment belongs to Him. He decides what is what. He is the Discriminator.

Then comes the intimate, existential message, as you would say. You will be returned to Him. In other words, you will enter the time-process and He will be present, you will go through the time-process and He will be present, and at your deathbed He will be nearer than the one near you. Then you will go into the grave and after that you will be returned to Him. That is the journey. That is the process.

Surat ar-Rahman (55:26-27):

$$ كُلُّ مَنْ عَلَيْهَا فَانٍ ۝ $$
$$ وَيَبْقَىٰ وَجْهُ رَبِّكَ ذُو الْجَلَالِ وَالْإِكْرَامِ ۝ $$

Everyone on it will pass away;
but the Face of your Lord will remain,
Master of Majesty and Generosity.

$$ كُلُّ مَنْ عَلَيْهَا فَانٍ ۝ $$

"Everyone on it will pass away"
is the reality of your life.

$$ وَيَبْقَىٰ وَجْهُ رَبِّكَ $$

"There will remain the Face of your Lord." Then it tells
us who our Lord is:

$$ ذُو الْجَلَالِ وَالْإِكْرَامِ ۝ $$

The Master of Majesty and Generosity. The One Who is the
Master of this whole situation is One of Majesty because of
the creation, and Generosity because of the creatures.

Surat Yunus (10:61):

وَمَا تَكُونُ فِى شَأْنٍ وَمَا تَتْلُوا مِنْهُ مِن
قُرْءَانٍ وَلَا تَعْمَلُونَ مِنْ عَمَلٍ إِلَّا كُنَّا عَلَيْكُمْ شُهُودًا إِذْ
تُفِيضُونَ فِيهِ ۚ وَمَا يَعْزُبُ عَن رَّبِّكَ مِن مِّثْقَالِ ذَرَّةٍ فِى الْأَرْضِ
وَلَا فِى السَّمَاءِ وَلَا أَصْغَرَ مِن ذَٰلِكَ وَلَا أَكْبَرَ إِلَّا فِى كِتَابٍ مُّبِينٍ ۞

You do not engage in any matter
or recite any of the Qur'an or do any action
without Our witnessing you
while you are occupied with it.
Not even the smallest speck eludes your Lord,
either on earth or in heaven.
Nor is there anything smaller than that, or larger,
which is not in a Clear Book.

You do not engage in any matter or recite any of the
Qur'an or do any action without Him witnessing you
while you are occupied with it. This is what is happening all the time. Allah says that He is witnessing us,
while we are busy doing these things. Existence is our
'busy doing that'. Reality is Allah watching you while
you are doing it. That was the famous Wird of Sahl at-
Tustari, the great Sufi of the East:

الله معي الله ناظر إليّ الله شاهد عليّ

Allah is with me, Allah sees me,
Allah is the Witness of my acts.

In case there is any doubt that Allah is generous, He

says: "Not even the smallest speck eludes your Lord either on earth or in heaven," there is no atom on the earth or in the sky but that it is known to Allah. "Nor is there anything smaller than that, or larger, which is not in a Clear Book." In other words, the mithal which Allah uses of the whole creation is this Book about which Rasul, sallallahu 'alayhi wa sallam, says, "The page is written and the ink is dry."

This is why Muslims cannot commit suicide thinking that they are somehow making things happen. They are in gross defiance of the Presence of Allah, subhanahu wa ta'ala. They have no permission to do such a thing, they have been ordered to worship, not to kill themselves, it is forbidden. They already have orders which are to fear Allah, not the enemy. It is of no use even to say that they do not fear death, because that is not what is happening at death as Allah, subhanahu wa ta'ala, has already explained: when you die, He is closer to you than the one watching you die. This is Whom you must fear, you must fear Allah.

Allah, subhanahu wa ta'ala, says: "There is not anything in it which is not in a Clear Book," which means from the mumin's point of view he says, "Alhamdulillah, we are safe. The foundations of our existence are secure. We are safe with Allah." Then you live your life knowing you are safe. This is the Yaqin which the Qur'an speaks about in varying degrees.

Now we will look at Surat Fussilat (41:53-54). Again Allah, subhanahu wa ta'ala, is challenging those ignorant people who do not get the point! If you do not have this knowledge of Tawhid, you do not know what life is about. You can only cause trouble and havoc. Allah says:

$$سَنُرِيهِمْ ءَايَٰتِنَا فِى ٱلْءَافَاقِ وَفِىٓ أَنفُسِهِمْ حَتَّىٰ يَتَبَيَّنَ لَهُمْ أَنَّهُ ٱلْحَقُّ ۗ أَوَلَمْ يَكْفِ بِرَبِّكَ أَنَّهُۥ عَلَىٰ كُلِّ شَىْءٍ شَهِيدٌ ۞ أَلَآ إِنَّهُمْ فِى مِرْيَةٍ مِّن لِّقَآءِ رَبِّهِمْ ۗ أَلَآ إِنَّهُۥ بِكُلِّ شَىْءٍ مُّحِيطٌۢ ۞$$

We will show them Our Signs on the horizon
and within themselves
until it is clear to them that it is the truth.
Is it not enough for your Lord
that He is a witness of everything?
What! Are they in doubt about
the meeting with their Lord?
What! Does He not encompass all things?

This is reiterating the ayat we saw earlier. "We will show them Our signs on the horizon," meaning in the world, "and inside themselves." In other words, Allah will indicate this matter that we have been looking at over the last couple of hours, in your lifetime, in what is going on out there and in what is going on in here. There will be signs, and what are the signs? The signs are evidences of the power of Allah, subhanahu wa ta'ala. What are the evidences of the power of Allah, subhanahu wa ta'ala? They are your recognising that you are dependent and He is Independent. You are the needy and He is the One

Who Provides. Therefore you do not need anything because He will provide for you. "We will show them Our
signs on the horizon and inside themselves until it is
clear to them that it is the truth."

$$أَوَلَمْ يَكْفِ بِرَبِّكَ أَنَّهُ عَلَىٰ كُلِّ شَيْءٍ شَهِيدٌ ۝$$

Is it not enough for your Lord that
He is a witness of everything?

This is the knowledge that matters. It is an experiential
knowledge that He is the Witness of everything. This is
the foundational reality of Tawhid. Allah, subhanahu wa
ta'ala, then connects that to:

$$أَلَا إِنَّهُمْ فِي مِرْيَةٍ مِّن لِّقَاءِ رَبِّهِمْ
وَأَلَا إِنَّهُ بِكُلِّ شَيْءٍ مُّحِيطٌ ۝$$

What! Are they in doubt
about the meeting with their Lord?
What! Does He not encompass all things?

This is the dividing line between the kuffar and the muminun. The muminun are those who are not in doubt
about the meeting with their Lord, and that is the evidence and proof because He has given signs throughout
their lifetime on the horizon and in themselves that confirm it. That is what Hajj is for. It is a sign on the horizon
because when you see the muminun, you do not have a
prayer at the Ka'aba or at Mina that is not also a prayer
for the dead.

Hajj is a sign on the horizon and there are signs in yourself because there are things Allah puts in the heart on Hajj that you cannot tell anybody. There are these millions of hajjis and they all have a secret from Allah in the Hajj. Everyone has something that happened with them that is not the thing they tell. This is the sign on the horizon and the sign in themselves. So they are not in doubt about the meeting with their Lord. That changes the person. The one who is not in doubt about the meeting with his Lord knows: "Does He not encompass all things?" That is what the Sufis call Hadrat ar-Rabbani, the Presence of Lordship. The heart begins to move in singing the Diwan, and from being solid, it is like you become opaque and these lights begin to come through and manifest and that is this Presence of Allah that is with us all the time, until the heart fills up with it and the eyes begin to fill with tears and all that is outside on the horizon becomes mixed up with all that is inside in the heart.

This is the beginning of the Tajalliyat, the illuminations from the Essence of Allah, subhanahu wa ta'ala, on the people of dhikr. This is why we meet, this is the purpose of what we are meeting for. This apparatus of knowledge becomes with us direct states of the heart and this is what Tasawwuf is, this is what the Tariqa is. It is because of our knowledge of Allah, subhanahu wa ta'ala, and our understanding of Qur'an, that we are able to experience these lights in the heart. Without this knowledge you could not experience these lights in the dhikr. Moulay al-'Arabi ad-Darqawi said, "My ecstasy, my drunkenness is in the discourse, not in the hadra."

V

APRIL 24TH 2004

We now come a step further from what we were doing at our last reunion. To recap, we will go to a couple of ayats which will confirm what we have already seen in the Qur'an. What we are coming to is an examination of an important term which is 'Tajalli.'

The proper understanding of Tawhid is the engagement of the slave with his Lord. You cannot have a Tawhid that does not have one who understands it. The fullness of the meaning of this unity of Allah, subhanahu wa ta'ala, involves the human creature entering into this stage of knowledge.

We will first look at Surat ar-Ra'd (13:33):

$$\text{أَفَمَنْ هُوَ قَآئِمٌ عَلَىٰ كُلِّ نَفْسٍ بِمَا كَسَبَتْ}$$

What then of Him Who is standing over every self
seeing everything it does?

We have to recognise, whether or not it is pleasing to
these modernists and scholars who think they can decide
what the doctrines of thinking in Islam are, that the
Qur'an is Clear, it is Mubin. "What then of Him Who is
standing over every self seeing everything it does?"
Therefore Allah, subhanahu wa ta'ala, Who is on the
Throne, Who governs the universe is, 'standing over
every self.' This is an extraordinary metaphor which
means He is dominating every self and seeing everything it does. This is the intellectual orientation of Iman
and the one who recognises this is established in Iman.

The question challenges the ignorant people who do not
understand the nature of existence, they are missing the
point of existence so their actions lead them and everyone else astray. The human creature is bonded to an ob-
ligation to his Lord to an understanding that He is a witness of his acts.

Now we go to Surat al-Hadid (57:3):

$$\text{هُوَ الْأَوَّلُ وَالْآخِرُ وَالظَّاهِرُ وَالْبَاطِنُ وَهُوَ بِكُلِّ شَيْءٍ عَلِيمٌ ۝}$$

He is the First and the Last,

the Outward and the Inward.
He has knowledge of all things.

This is the famous ayat we all know and which encompasses everything of creation – firstness and lastness, outwardness and inwardness, that is time and space. Huwal-Awwalu wal-Akhiru – all the measure of time, the in-time from its beginning to the in-time at its end. Huwadh-Dhahiru wal-Batin – all the outsideness of things and all the insideness of things.

Look at how Allah, subhanahu wa ta'ala, specifically relates particular Attributes of His in explaining His reality to the human creatures. "He has knowledge of all things" – this is an Attribute of Allah, subhanahu wa ta'ala. So all the in-time things are in His present knowledge, His continuous knowledge, His absolute knowledge and there is nothing hidden from Him. Also, He has knowledge of all the outward of things and all the inward of things, and as we saw earlier He knows what is in the breast.

This is an absolute confirmation of the reality of Allah, subhanahu wa ta'ala, and there is nothing excluded, there is nothing outside of that. All of the creational realities therefore are declaring the Presence of Allah, subhanahu wa ta'ala. One of the shuyukh of the East, Al-Iraqi said, "How can love deny there is nothing in existence except Him?" This is where the kuffar, who do not want to face up to this, say that we equate Allah with the universe, that Allah is the universe. But what we are saying is that the existent things have no reality in themselves, therefore they are masiwallah, other-than-Allah, therefore they are non-existent.

"How can love deny there is nothing in existence except Him?" So the reality of existence is Allah, but again we are stuck at a point which seems to have no exit. We have established that existence belongs to Allah alone. Attributes and Actions must be His also because Allah is One in His Essence, His Attributes – seeing, knowing, hearing, doing – and Actions must be His also because the attributes of these faculties cannot themselves manifest without an action. You cannot have seeing and knowing and hearing and doing and speech without action, and action belongs to Allah, subhanahu wa ta'ala.

He has firstness and lastness, outsideness and insideness, and these relations are established with the essences of things. In other words, we have sight, we have knowledge, we have hearing, we have seeing – the essences of the things, of the creatures have these faculties but we do not have anything, we are not existent, only Allah is the existent. These essences of the things are subsistent in Allah's knowledge. Our reality comes by being existent in the knowledge of Allah. The created things are the result of the Divine 'kun!' emerging from the inward to the outward and they are other-than-Allah. All the created things are masiwallah.

Allah's Dhat, the Essence of Allah is not like anything, free from the determinations of the essences of things. Allah is not like the created creatures. We have essence, we have attributes, we have action but He is not connected to us.

Now we look at Surat an-Nahl (16:3). We still have to get out of this dilemma about our non-existence and yet our having these attributes that Allah, subhanahu wa ta'ala, has.

$$\text{خَلَقَ السَّمَوٰتِ وَالْأَرْضَ بِالْحَقِّ}$$
$$\text{تَعٰلٰى عَمَّا يُشْرِكُونَ ۝}$$

He created the heavens and the earth with truth.
He is exalted above anything they associate with Him.

You must concentrate very hard now, and you will understand it very clearly. "He created the heavens and the earth with truth," 'bil-Haqq'. Here Allah opens the door on the very core of this understanding of Tawhid.

We have established this dilemma that we have the attributes that Allah claims to be uniquely His and yet we somehow have an in-time experience of them – we see, we hear, we know, we judge, we act – but Allah has revealed here that He has created the heavens and the earth bil-Haqq, with the Truth. So there is not a connection, but it is how things are that all these created forms which have no existence in themselves, which are utterly dependent on Allah, subhanahu wa ta'ala, are nevertheless created bil-Haqq.

Allah will open out to us now what the nature of this bil-Haqq is, and again, without this you cannot have Tawhid.

$$\text{تَعٰلٰى عَمَّا يُشْرِكُونَ ۝}$$

He is raised above anything they associate with Him.

Allah is locking us into this stage of knowledge because
we have to admit that He created the heavens and the
earth bil-Haqq and at the same time He is exalted above
the things. So it is still this impossible, apparent contradiction because He is exalted above everything they
associate with Allah and what can you associate with
Allah except the things, except the created existence?

Let us continue with discovering the Qur'anic ayats. We
have to go to Surat Ta Ha (20:114):

$$\text{فَتَعَـٰلَى ٱللَّهُ ٱلْمَلِكُ ٱلْحَقُّ}$$

High exalted be Allah, the King, the Real!

Allah says He is exalted, He is raised above all the created
forms and He says He is the King, which means He rules
over all the created forms. Also He is Al-Haqq, the Real.
The mutakallimun have always recognised that this name
Al-Haqq is used very specially by Allah in the Qu'ran
and it relates to the Essence, the Dhat of Allah. So the
very Essence of Allah, the unknowable, the unthinkable,
that on which you cannot meditate or try to grasp – the
very core of the Divine Reality – is the Ruler Who is
exalted above everything.

Now we go back to Surat ad-Dukhan (44:39):

$$\text{مَا خَلَقْنَـٰهُمَآ إِلَّا بِٱلْحَقِّ}$$

We did not create them except with Haqq.

– so the created forms have been created from the very Essence of Him Who is exalted above all the things. Then He says,

وَلَٰكِنَّ أَكْثَرَهُمْ لَا يَعْلَمُونَ ۝

But most of them do not know it.

– most of the human creatures do not know this. This is also true of those Muslims who have abandoned the proper teaching of Islam which has remained constant from the beginning and has been in the hands of very respected and noble 'ulama. It is only in the last one hundred and fifty years that this whole understanding collapsed. The interesting thing is that the understanding of this highest aspect of the Deen went along with that thing which sustained the whole of the Deen throughout the whole of society, which is the Amr of Shari'ah. When the Amr was removed by which the Shari'ah was imposed, then the understanding of Tawhid went. These things are not disconnected.

Allah says:

مَا خَلَقْنَٰهُمَا إِلَّا بِالْحَقِّ وَلَٰكِنَّ أَكْثَرَهُمْ لَا يَعْلَمُونَ ۝

We did not create them except with truth,
but most of them do not know it.

The loss of the Amr was the abandoning of the Tawhid.

They could not have abandoned the Shari'ah if they had not lost the doctrine, the understanding of Tawhid. Therefore the responsibility for the disappearance of the leaders of the Muslims comes back on the common people who had been given this knowledge and who let it slip out of their fingers.

Now we go to Surat Yunus (10:5 and 6):

خَلَقَ ٱللَّهُ ذَٰلِكَ إِلَّا بِٱلْحَقِّ نُفَصِّلُ ٱلْآيَٰتِ لِقَوْمٍ يَعْلَمُونَ ۝ إِنَّ فِي ٱخْتِلَٰفِ ٱلَّيْلِ وَٱلنَّهَارِ وَمَا خَلَقَ ٱللَّهُ فِي ٱلسَّمَٰوَٰتِ وَٱلْأَرْضِ لَآيَٰتٍ لِّقَوْمٍ يَتَّقُونَ ۝

Allah did not create these things except with truth.
We make the Signs clear for people who know.
In the alternation of night and day
and what Allah has created in the heavens and the earth
there are Signs for people who have taqwa.

Allah, subhanahu wa ta'ala, gives another chance, another possibility to grasp this tremendous thing that we are moving towards understanding.

"Allah did not create these things except with truth." We have established this, we have understood this. After that Allah says: "We make the Signs clear for people who know." 'Sign' is a very important word in the Qur'an which appears throughout the Qur'an in delineating the people of knowledge from the ignorant, that is the muminun from the kafirun. "We make the Signs clear for people who know." Remember that elsewhere Allah says: "There are signs in your self and on the horizon." Therefore a sign is an indicator and these signs have been created to give us an understanding of how existence is.

"We make the Signs clear for people who know," and the people who know are the people who glorify Allah, subhanahu wa ta'ala, because they have not been created except to glorify Him, subhanahu wa ta'ala. If they have knowledge it is because they worship Him, if they do not worship Him then they do not have knowledge of Him. The matter is not one of ratiocination, it is not one of reason, but one of seeing clearly.

Knowing is by confirmation – "We make the Signs clear for people who know." Then Allah indicates the sign:

إِنَّ فِي اخْتِلَافِ الَّيْلِ وَالنَّهَارِ
وَمَا خَلَقَ اللَّهُ فِي السَّمَوَاتِ وَالْأَرْضِ

In the alternation of night and day
and what Allah has created
in the heavens and the earth.

The alternation of night and day means that this planet is moving in its orbit with a sun and a moon, and this regulates our existence on the earth. It is measured, it has order, everything is in its place. Our reality is based on the continuous flow of the time-process which only exists because the sun is there illuminating the earth, 'setting' – going out of our sight, and coming back into our sight with the day. These are signs which indicate the purposefulness, the meaningfulness of existence in the alternation of the night and day.

$$\text{وَمَا خَلَقَ اللَّهُ فِي السَّمَوَاتِ وَالْأَرْضِ}$$

And what Allah has created in the heavens and earth.

– which therefore means that if you look out further beyond our immediate reality on earth with the sun and the moon, out to the stars, in all of this Allah then indicates the key of this knowing – the knowing clicks into something else. It is not knowing by the intellect, by measuring, it is knowing these are: "Signs for people who have taqwa." If you realise the power of Allah, subhanahu wa ta'ala, you change. This taqwa is something natural and connects to fitra. If you go to people who have not had the word of Islam, by their fitra they are in some way acknowledging their recognition of the movement of the stars. The people who have examined the ancient stone edifices of ancient peoples see that they have connected their understanding to the knowledge of the movement of the stars. It is an awareness of the harmony of the universe and this is from taqwa. Taqwa is therefore the foundation of knowledge. The person with taqwa is another kind of person, and this is the mumin. We are now moving closer.

We go to Surat al-'Ankabut (29:44):

$$\text{خَلَقَ ٱللَّهُ ٱلسَّمَـٰوَٰتِ وَٱلۡأَرۡضَ بِٱلۡحَقِّ}$$
$$\text{إِنَّ فِى ذَٰلِكَ لَأٓيَةً لِّلۡمُؤۡمِنِينَ ﴿﴾}$$

Allah created the heavens and the earth with truth.
There is certainly a Sign in that for the muminun.

Now it is clear. Grasping this is an important indication
that Allah has deemed necessary to mention who it is for.
It is for the muminun. The ones who know are the ones
who have taqwa and the ones who have taqwa are the
muminun, the people who have Iman in Allah, subhanahu wa ta'ala. The Dhat, the Essence of Allah, is present
in both the origination of the world and in its continuance. We have established that Allah is the Outward,
because, "He has created the heavens and the earth bil-
Haqq," and this is a sign for the muminun.

Now we go to Surat an-Nur (24:25):

$$\text{وَيَعۡلَمُونَ أَنَّ ٱللَّهَ هُوَ ٱلۡحَقُّ ٱلۡمُبِينُ ﴿٢٥﴾}$$

And they will know that Allah is the Clear Truth.

Now it is all being laid out. They will know that Allah
is the Haqq al-Mubin, the Clear Truth, the Manifest
Truth. They will know, and this is the knowledge that
He says will come to the human creature, that Allah is
manifest, clear Haqq – Essence, unknowable, exalted
above everything they associate with Him. So the Dhat
of Allah is present in the creation of the world and in the
continuance of the world.

We stay with Surat an-Nur, ayat 35.

$$ اَللَّهُ نُورُ السَّمَوَٰتِ وَالْاَرْضِ $$

Allah is the Light of the heavens and the earth.

We are being taken further into the secret of existence. Further we find:

$$ يَهْدِے اللَّهُ لِنُورِهِۦ مَن يَشَآءُ $$

Allah guides to His Light whomever He wills.

So Allah is the Light of the heavens and the earth and He will guide to His Light whomever He wants. We have established that Allah is One in His Acts, His Attributes and His Essence, unalterable, and He manifests Himself through His Attribute of light in the forms of the created objects, which in reality are only reflected entities because they have no existence in themselves. They are made bil-Haqq, so they are a reflection of what is true, manifesting outwardly the essences which are in the knowledge of Allah. So the Divine Qualities emerge in the world of created phenomena. In other words, the human creature has knowledge, will, seeing, hearing, power and action reflected on him by this light from the Essence of Allah, subhanahu wa ta'ala, on His Throne.

Remember that things are not and cannot be created out of nothing. "Nothing can come of nothing," as Shakespeare said. Equally non-being cannot manifest as the matter of being on the form of beings, so a nothing cannot make things happen. Allah is above all limitation and all individuation, and yet this happens by His Light. Allah reveals Himself in the objects in accordance with the essences of the things which He has created by His knowledge. They have these characteristics of knowing, seeing, willing, by His knowledge.

Allah, subhanahu wa ta'ala, has shown Himself in the objects in accordance with the essences of the things, hidden in His Essence and subsisting in His Attribute of knowledge. It is by His knowledge that He lets these things come into being. They are brought out by His Action: "Kun!" He only has to say to a thing, "Kun!" and it is.

The khalq, the created things come into created manifestation by the manifesting of Allah, subhanahu wa ta'ala, by His name Al-Khaliq. The Creator is an Attribute of the One Who is Reality, is Essence, is Haqq, high exalted above everything they could connect with Him. The famous Jami said: "Essences of the creatures are mirrors wherein Allah reflects Himself. Or, Allah's Being is the mirror wherein the essences reflect their forms." The Shaykh al-Akbar Ibn al-'Arabi said: "Allah is your mirror wherein you see yourself, and you are His mirror wherein He sees His own Names and their working."

Shaykh Ibn al-'Arabi says, "Were He not and were we not, what has happened would not have happened." Thus our existence is due to Him and His manifestation, His Tajalli is due to us. It is due to us that this manifestation takes place. He is the Rich, the Independent and we are the poor, the utterly dependent.

VI

MAY 1ST 2004

I will just recapitulate the summing-up of the point we got to last week. We quoted Shaykh al-Akbar Ibn al-'Arabi as saying: "Were He not and were we not, what has happened would not have happened." There he is declaring the foundational reality in which we find ourselves. From it we derive that our existence is due to Him and His manifestation is due to us. Thus He is the Rich and Independent, and we are the poor and utterly dependent.

We summed up that Allah the Powerful, the Immutable, without change or multiplicity, without hulul – without embodiment in any form, or ittihad – without joining to anything, and without division, He manifests Himself by what we took as a technical term, al-'Ayan ath-Thabita, by His source-forms through His Attribute of light. The countless variety of source-forms that come into creation do not affect the unity of Allah and His being beyond them.

We have come to this key word which is 'Tajalli'. It is a Qur'anic term which means 'manifestation' or 'revelation', 'revealing of itself.' For there to be a Tajalli from Allah, subhanahu wa ta'ala, this requires a form. There cannot be a manifestation unless it becomes manifest so these forms are in the knowledge of Allah, but they have no intrinsic reality. Yet things do not come out of absolute nothingness, they come out of the nothing which is the zone of His knowledge of the forms which will manifest. We have to make this distinction.

To understand the nature of this manifesting we will look at Surat al-A'raf (7:143):

وَلَمَّا جَاءَ مُوسَىٰ لِمِيقَٰتِنَا وَكَلَّمَهُ رَبُّهُ قَالَ رَبِّ أَرِنِىٓ أَنظُرْ إِلَيْكَ قَالَ لَن تَرَىٰنِى وَلَٰكِنِ ٱنظُرْ إِلَى ٱلْجَبَلِ فَإِنِ ٱسْتَقَرَّ مَكَانَهُ فَسَوْفَ تَرَىٰنِى فَلَمَّا تَجَلَّىٰ رَبُّهُ لِلْجَبَلِ جَعَلَهُ دَكًّا وَخَرَّ مُوسَىٰ صَعِقًا فَلَمَّآ أَفَاقَ قَالَ سُبْحَٰنَكَ تُبْتُ إِلَيْكَ وَأَنَا۠ أَوَّلُ ٱلْمُؤْمِنِينَ ۝

When Musa came into Our appointed time
and His Lord spoke to him,
he said, 'My Lord, show me Yourself
so that I may look at You!'
He said, 'You will not see me
but look at the mountain.
If it remains firm in its place,
then you will see Me.'
But when his Lord manifested Himself to the mountain,
He crushed it flat
and Musa fell unconscious to the ground.
When he regained consciousness he said,
'Glory be to You! I make tawba to You
and I am the first of the muminun.'

وَلَمَّا جَآءَ مُوسَىٰ لِمِيقَٰتِنَا

When Musa came into Our appointed time.

Look at how Allah surrounds the whole event, how He is the author of the event. It is an unfolding in itself of the point at which, as it were, the fixing of the Nabawiyya of Sayyiduna Musa takes place. 'Our appointed time' is Allah's appointment of him as a Messenger.

وَكَلَّمَهُ رَبُّهُ

His Lord spoke to him

– Allah spoke to Sayyiduna Musa because this is part of the Maqam of the Messengers, that they are spoken to by Allah, subhanahu wa ta'ala.

119

$$\text{قَالَ رَبِّ أَرِنِي}$$

He said, 'My Lord, show me Yourself!'

What is amazing is that there are these things in the Qur'an, and there are these ignorant, untaught 'ulama who have not been taught to reflect on the nature of Tawhid, and have not been able to confront that Sayyiduna Musa says: "My Lord, show me Yourself." This is what is called the Maqam al-Uns, the Station of Intimacy. In an intimacy with his Lord he speaks freely to Him. You will also find in all the recounting of the Mi'raj this intimacy with which Rasul, sallallahu 'alayhi wa sallam, speaks openly to his Lord. "My Lord, show me Yourself so that I may look at You." This is the Station of Intimacy, of love. The lover wants to look on the Face of the Beloved.

$$\text{قَالَ لَنْ تَرَانِي وَلَٰكِنِ انْظُرْ إِلَى الْجَبَلِ}$$

Allah, subhanahu wa ta'ala, says: "You will not see Me," and remember this in what we are coming to later – then He takes him into the station of Ma'rifa. He says: "But look at the mountain." The mountain is the most unarguable evidence of the khalq, of the created, it is solid rock.

$$\text{فَإِنِ اسْتَقَرَّ مَكَانَهُ فَسَوْفَ تَرَانِي}$$

"If it remains firm in its place then You will see Me." He has asked for this to happen and Allah, subhanahu wa ta'ala, orders him to look at the mountain, at the created form.

VI

$$\text{فَلَمَّا تَجَلَّىٰ رَبُّهُۥ لِلْجَبَلِ جَعَلَهُۥ دَكًّا}$$

"But when His Lord manifested Himself," when His Lord made this Tajalli, which is the word we have been looking at – "When His Lord manifested Himself to the mountain He crushed it flat."

This event was the illumination, the opening, the fatiha of Sayyiduna Musa, 'alayhi salam. What did it mean? From the outside we can say this: the mountain was still there but Allah, subhanahu wa ta'ala, had taken the form from the mountain so that all that was left was the dust. "Huwal-Awwalu wal-Akhiru, wadh-Dhahiru wal-Batin." Sayyiduna Musa realised that Allah is the Creator of the Dhahir and that He had removed the source-form which Allah had in His knowledge, so the thing was reduced to dust. It did not disappear, it was not magic, but the form was gone. He realised that all the projections of the created universe are themselves manifestations of Allah, subhanahu wa ta'ala. So when Allah manifested to the mountain He crushed it flat.

$$\text{وَخَرَّ مُوسَىٰ صَعِقًا}$$

And Musa fell unconscious to the ground.

This is taken among the teachers of Tasawwuf to be an open description of what the Sufis call 'fana fillah'. Sayyiduna Musa was annihilated in this knowledge of Allah's revelation. Moulay al-'Arabi ad-Darqawi said: "If the world disappears, Allah has to appear." Of course Allah is not compelled to anything, but what he meant was that in the wisdom of how He has set up existence, if the world disappears, Allah has to appear because He is the Haqq. When the Tajalliyat of the solid forms vanish, then Allah is manifest. Allah says in Surat an-Nur (24:35):

$$\text{ٱللَّهُ نُورُ ٱلسَّمَٰوَٰتِ وَٱلۡأَرۡضِ}$$

Allah is the Light of the heavens and the earth.

Then Sayyiduna Musa returns to consciousness. This next part of the ayat, in the language of the Sufis, is 'baqa billah'. He does not return exalted, thinking that he has some secret knowledge. He returns completely, utterly reduced to being the first of the muminun and he says:

$$\text{سُبۡحَٰنَكَ}$$

"Glory be to You." First he exalts Allah, subhanahu wa ta'ala, he makes tasbih. Then he makes tawba:

$$\text{تُبۡتُ إِلَيۡكَ}$$

I make tawba to You.

He is the Messenger of Allah, subhanahu wa ta'ala, and he makes tawba to Allah, he asks forgiveness. He even asks forgiveness for his adab that he should have asked that he could have the vision of Allah.

$$\text{وَأَنَا۠ أَوَّلُ ٱلۡمُؤۡمِنِينَ ۝}$$

I am the first of the muminun.

This is the declaration of Sayyiduna Musa that he has accepted the destiny of being the Messenger of Allah, subhanahu wa ta'ala. In saying, "I am the first of the muminun," he is saying 'I have taken on this task you have given me. I am the Messenger of Allah.' All this is in this event of this Tajalli from the Essence of Allah, subhanahu wa ta'ala.

We will go now to the Diwan of Shaykh Muhammad ibn al-Habib, rahimahullah, to the qasida called The Buraq of the Tariq. Our Shaykh says:

وَالْحَقُّ لَا يُرَى فِي غَيْرِ مَظْهَرِ   لِأَحَدٍ مِــنْ مَلَكٍ أَوْ بَشَرِ

فَالْمَظْهَرُ الأَوَّلُ نُـــورُ أَحْمَدَا   عَلَيْهِ أَفْضَلُ الصَّلَاةِ سَرْمَدَا

The Haqq can only be seen in manifestation,
whether by an angel or a mortal man.

The first manifestation of the light
is the light of Ahmad,
may the most excellent of blessings
be upon him eternally.

Now we go to the Lesser Qasida where our Shaykh says:

وَلَيْسَ يُرَى الرَّحْمانُ إِلاَّ فِي مَظْهَرِ   كَعَرْشٍ وَكُرْسِيٍّ وَلَـــوْحٍ وَسِدْرَةِ

The Merciful is only to be seen in manifestations like the Throne, the Footstool, the Tablet or the Lote-Tree.

Again, what is being said in the Diwan is being echoed from what we have found in the Qur'an. The Tajalli comes but only allowing the creature to see that the manifestation of the Essence is the manifestation of the power of Allah, subhanahu wa ta'ala, in these forms which are the limit-forms of creational knowledge.

These two things have come together which we looked at at the beginning and established ruthlessly as separate. We have on the one hand this term of the mutakallimun, of the Sufis, which is the 'Tanzih Mutlaq'. This is absolute transcendence. 'Tanzih' is that nothing can be associated with Allah, subhanahu wa ta'ala. At the same time we have Tashbih, which is that there is an imminence, a Presence of Allah, subhanahu wa ta'ala, in manifestation. They are created forms but as we saw earlier, "We have created everything bil-Haqq," they are not illusion.

Shaykh al-Akbar said very beautifully, "If you assert only Tanzih," which is like the wahhabis, that He is above all and has absolutely no connection with the creation at all, "you limit Allah." Because you are still left with this enormous creation. "If you assert only Tashbih," in other words, like the pantheists who say that Allah is in the universe, in all the stuff, "then you define Him." So if you exalt Him above the creation you limit Him, and if you declare He is in it, you define Him. "But if you assert both, you follow the right course and you are a leader and master in Ma'rifa."

The Dhat of Allah, the Essence of Allah, the Haqq, is existent. The dhat, the essences of the created things are

non-existent but we have established that when we say
'non-existence' it is a relative non-existence because nothing can come out of nothing. It comes out of what is
in the knowledge of Allah, subhanahu wa ta'ala, without
diminishing or being connected to it.

Thus from the point of view of essences, otherness is
predicated from the beginning to the end. All the essences of the created things are masiwallah, other-than-
Allah. The known of Allah, from eternity, is still other-
than-Allah. They are knowledges, but they are not the
'He-ness' of Him. The Essence is still immutable, un-
touched. These known things are known in His knowledge just as, to take a metaphor, you can know about
someone somewhere and visualise them, but it does not
diminish you or add to you. There are signs in yourself
and on the horizon if you only understand. The creation
is not connected to Allah, it is utterly dependent on
Allah. Without Him it cannot be and He is independent
of everything.

From the point of view of the essences, otherness is real.
From the point of view of Existence, of Being, of the
Divine – identity is real. Surat al-Ikhlas:

بِسْمِ اللهِ الرَّحْمٰنِ الرَّحِيمِ

قُلْ هُوَ اللهُ أَحَدٌ ۟ اللهُ الصَّمَدُ ۟ لَمْ يَلِدْ
وَلَمْ يُولَدْ ۟ وَلَمْ يَكُنْ لَهُ كُفُوًا أَحَدٌ ۟

In the name of Allah, All-Merciful, Most Merciful

"Say: 'He is Allah, Absolute Oneness,
Allah, the Everlasting Sustainer of all.
He has not given birth and was not born.
And no one is comparable to Him.'"

The existence of the Haqq is nothing but the existence of the created beings. That is, the One is revealing Itself in the forms of the essences of the created things. Otherness and identity. The oneness of Allah and the otherness of all the created things. We understand with a double knowledge this Tawhid which is One.

Shah Kamaluddin said: "To soar into the realms of Ma'rifa, develop the two wings of identity and otherness." The created things are other-than-Allah and Allah has identity with a knowledge that encompasses all the created things.

We have come to four terms which will clear this up for us. The one who sees only the phenomenal, the created stuff, otherness, is veiled. He is called mahjoub. He who identifies the phenomenal with the Haqq, the one who says: "God is in the world, He is actually the world," is an illusionist. He is called maghzoub. He who is intoxicated with the wine of unity, who says: "There is only Allah!" is drunk with Allah. He is an absorbtionist absorbed in the majesty of Allah, and is called majdhoub. But he who distinguishes between otherness, the creation, and identity, the Creator, is loved by Him. He is mahboub.

So you have four – the mahjoub, the maghzoub, the majdhoub and the mahboub. The first sees only otherness and he is veiled, mahjoub. He is a materialist. The one who identifies the phenomena with the haqq is a maghzoub. The one who is intoxicated with the wine of His unity, he is absorbed in the Divine and is an absorbtionist and is majdhoub. But the one who distinguishes between otherness and identity is loved by Him and is mahboub. These are the four states of knowledge.

The first one is kufr itself. The other two are those who have been led astray, and the one who is on the Sirat al-Mustaqim is the one who distinguishes between otherness and identity.

To see this in its clearest form we will go to Surat ar-Rahman (55:19-21).

مَرَجَ الْبَحْرَيْنِ يَلْتَقِيَانِ ۝ بَيْنَهُمَا بَرْزَخٌ لَا يَبْغِيَانِ ۝
فَبِأَيِّ ءَالَآءِ رَبِّكُمَا تُكَذِّبَانِ ۝

He has let loose the two seas, converging together,
with a barrier between them
they do not break through.
So which of your Lord's blessings
do you both then deny?

This is the summing up of this matter. Allah, subhanahu wa ta'ala, has set up existence with these two seas. They come together, but there is a barrier between them which does not break. Allah is the Rabb and the slave is the slave. Allah is the Creator and the creation is the creation. Until you say these two things you do not have a pure Tawhid. Then Allah, subhanahu wa ta'ala, asks:

$$ فَبِأَيِّ ءَالَآءِ رَبِّكُمَا تُكَذِّبَانِ ۝ $$

So which of your Lord's blessings
do you both then deny?

Do you deny the blessings of His being exalted above the creation, or do you deny the blessings of this enormous universe that He has made for us? This is the true understanding of Tawhid and it is embedded in this blessed ayat of Surat ar-Rahman.

HADRA

We make du'a to Allah, subhanahu wa ta'ala, to make from among this gathering of people the Awliya and salihun who will take the message of Islam through the whole of this continent. We ask Allah, subhanahu wa ta'ala, that by the people of this gathering the Deen of Islam will stretch from the south and raise its hand up to the north to restore Islam to the Berber and Arab people.

We ask Allah, subhanahu wa ta'ala, to give a fatiha to all the people of this gathering, and give them a fatiha for their own ruhani knowledge and for their actions in the world. We ask Allah, subhanahu wa ta'ala, to give light and strength and inspiration to all the people gathered here.

We ask Allah, subhanahu wa ta'ala, to let love grow in

the hearts of the fuqara. We ask Allah, subhanahu wa
ta'ala, to make this a group of people worthy of the company of the Sahaba. We ask Allah, subhanahu wa ta'ala,
to make them the Sahaba of their time. We ask Allah,
subhanahu wa ta'ala, to raise this Tariqa up to be a light
for the whole of Africa.

سُبْحَانَ رَبِّكَ رَبِّ الْعِزَّةِ عَمَّا يَصِفُونَ ۝ وَسَلَامٌ عَلَى الْمُرْسَلِينَ ۝ وَالْحَمْدُ لِلَّهِ رَبِّ الْعَالَمِينَ ۝

VII

MAY 8TH 2004

We have been going step by step in an unfolding of something. When you have assimilated all of this you will be among the knowers of Allah, subhanahu wa ta'ala. You will be among the people of knowledge and you will have entered into an understanding of Tawhid which is the Tawhid of the elite.

There is the Tawhid of the common people, the Tawhid of the elite, and there is the Tawhid of the elect of the elite. You have to grasp each stage of the way we have been going as each stage is an unfolding which will take you to another station of understanding and knowledge.

We were looking at how we can understand Allah the Creator, and creation. We looked at how the things come into being. We confirmed the oneness of Allah and at the same time we recognised that the created things were made bil-Haqq, by the Truth. We saw that there has to be a double understanding of Allah as the Outward and the Inward, and His relationship to the creation.

Now we are going to look at two terms which are, as it were, in the courtesy of how we may talk about Allah, subhanahu wa ta'ala. They are called Tanzih and Tashbih, and they are opposites.

Tanzih is exaltation. Allah is exalted above everything that can be associated with Him. Tanzih is disconnection. Allah is disconnected from the forms. Tashbih is when there are modes of speaking about Allah, subhanahu wa ta'ala, which seem to imply that He has form in the world of forms in time. We have to understand how this is so that we have a proper understanding of it.

Everything we have done so far has been founded on the teachings of Al-Ash'ari. He is a kind of defence system to prevent the rationalists and philosophers breaking down the barriers of adab and courtesy to the understanding of the Divine, and to prevent the reduction of our understanding of the Divine to a level of thought, to ideas and philosophy.

The Sufis go further. They do not negate Al-Ash'ari, in fact it is necessary to understand him because he is the one who speaks about the Acts, the Attributes and the

Essence of Allah, subhanahu wa ta'ala. Now we are going to go past that, we are going to vault over it without denying it in any way, to arrive at an understanding of these two terms which you might say are 'connection' and 'disconnection' – a way of speaking about Allah that appears in the Qur'an which seems to connect Him to the forms, and disconnecting Allah from the forms. We are going to do this in such a manner that we arrive at a knowledge of Allah, subhanahu wa ta'ala, in which there is no iota of association of Allah with anything.

We are going to look at Tashbih, this connection of Allah, subhanahu wa ta'ala, to created forms. We go first to Surat an-Najm (53:8-9):

$$ \text{ثُمَّ دَنَا فَتَدَلَّىٰ ۝ فَكَانَ قَابَ قَوْسَيْنِ أَوْ أَدْنَىٰ ۝} $$

Then he drew near and hung suspended.
He was two bow-lengths away
or even closer.

Here we have a statement in the Qur'an of Rasul, sallallahu 'alayhi wa sallam, drawing near and being two bow-lengths away or even closer, meaning he was two bow-lengths away from Allah, subhanahu wa ta'ala. This statement flies in the face of all that we have been looking at because first of all it implies that this nearness is an actual, physical drawing near in this apparent proximity which implies space and time.

To understand this we must look at this statement of "two bow-lengths or even closer." We know that the Arab kings in the old days would let those brought nearest to them only approach to the length of two bows. That was as near the subject could approach the ruler. Intellectual proof which we have already established negates limit and distance from Allah so we have to find out how we are going to understand this statement.

You must know that that sect in Arabia, which has destroyed great swathes of the Deen and great swathes of the Muslims, has taught for some considerable time that for them this was a physical reality. The famous Ibn Batutta tells that he heard Ibn Taymiyya talking, astagh-firullah, about Allah, subhanahu wa ta'ala, descending from the Throne, "As I descend from this mimbar." In other words, they are anthropomorphists. They see the Divine as a being and an entity, and this is what is taught in Arabia where people are blowing everybody up including themselves.

Let us look at this. The Qur'an is Mubin. It is a Clear Qur'an which has been revealed in a clear Arabic. Remember that the Arabic language was prepared for the Qur'an, the Qur'an was not prepared to fit into the Arabic language. Allah, subhanahu wa ta'ala, prepared the Arabic language over centuries, took it to a point of fineness, refined it, extended it, made it more precise, then He gave to the Quraish tribe the gift of the best Arabic tongue. Then from the Quraish He gave to one family the exact pronunciation so that the Rasul, sallallahu 'alayhi wa sallam, said about his family: "We have been given the Dhad." They are the one family who were given the pure pronunciation of the letter Dhad.

So the language was perfected in his family so that at the time the Revelation came it was in this pure Arabic. So specific is it that Allah then permitted it to stretch over different readings so that there would be no ambiguity in it. At the same time it would be like one diamond that has different facets, so light would come from different ways, so that different readings illuminate the Qur'an in different ways, without them contradicting what was intended in the message of the Qur'an.

Rasul, sallallahu 'alayhi wa sallam, not only spoke it in this perfect family Arabic, he also spoke it in what you might call dialects, so that his followers could understand.

In Arabic there are four classes of phrase. If you look at the books of Arabic grammar like the famous Ajrumiyya and so on, you find for example that the great Sufi of Morocco, Shaykh Ibn 'Ajiba, has written a Sufic commentary on the Ajrumiyya, giving a different spiritual meaning and emphasis to every possible grammatical construct. The language is very formal and structured and can be appreciated in this way.

In Arabic there are four classes of phrase, of expression. There is a 'clear phrase': "The sea, key, scissors." There are 'indicated phrases' which have an agreed definition: if you say, "Man," we all know what that means, if you say, "Woman," or "Bird," we know what that means. It is an indicated phrase which represents some genus of which all are the same.

Then there are 'shared phrases' which have two meanings. For example, the word 'ayn in Arabic means 'eye', and it also means a 'spring.' Insan means 'man' and it also means the 'pupil of the eye.' This particular shared phrase is of vital importance to the way of speaking which is used by Shaykh al-Akbar because he sees a very important meaning in the fact that insan represents man and it also represents the pupil of the eye. So the shared phrase has two meanings at the same time.

Then we have the 'synonym phrase'. For example, the different words for lion like asad and hizaba, or for sword like sayf and husam – different words meaning the same thing.

In Arabic these four are defined as the four matrices. They are to language what the hot, the cold, the wet and the dry are to nature – they are fundamental. From these come other expressions: the simile, the metaphor, and transmitted phrases, phrases that are passed down.

If you take the simile, this sounds like something which is different from the four matrices. If you say something is "like light," it is applied to the known. But 'like light' is with the eye in revealing the sensory object which is seen. 'Like light' also means that the eye is able to see the thing it sees because you cannot say, "like light" if you are not able to see the object by the light. Then you say that knowledge is called light. For this process to happen you have a knowledge, and then this knowledge is called light so it becomes the third matrix, it becomes the shared phrase. All phrases move towards one of these four matrices.

'Like light' is a simile because in fact it moves to the shared phrase and means two things at once. Once you say, "This is like light," you have given two meanings at the same time. You cannot say, "Like light" without saying therefore that it is illuminating and therefore it is knowledge. So the understanding of it and the seeing of it are not disconnected but connected. Your grasping 'like light' is also your recognition of something. If you make a simile it is 'like light' but your knowing what is meant by 'like light' is knowledge, so it is both 'like light' and a knowledge which comes from this.

The 'Arif recognises what the Divine Presence demands: purity, disconnection and negation of likeness. These are not veiled by reports of Allah using the tools of limitation by time, direction and place. So the meaning – because we know that Allah is disconnected from everything – moves from one to the other so that we go back to the ayat: "Then he drew near and hung suspended. He was two bow-lengths away or even closer." But Allah is pure, disconnected and has no likeness.

The meaning moves from the report to the reality. It moves from the Mulk to the Malakut, it moves from the kingdom of forms to the Unseen. Let us be patient. A slave-girl was brought to the Rasul, sallallahu 'alayhi wa sallam, and they said about her, "This slave-girl is mushrik, she is connecting things to Allah." Rasul said, "Bring her to me!" And he said to the girl, "Where is Allah?" and the slave-girl pointed to the sky. The Messenger had better knowledge of Allah than her yet he affirmed her belief, and Allah has better knowledge of

Himself, disconnected from all forms.

Rasul, sallallahu 'alayhi wa sallam, knew that "Where is Allah?" is a question you cannot ask, and she gave an answer which on the face of it, you cannot give. But she pointed to the sky which is undifferentiated, it has no form, it is just blue and Rasul said, "She is mumin."

We go to Surat al-Mulk (67:16-17):

$$\text{ءَأَمِنتُم مَّن فِي السَّمَاءِ أَن يَخْسِفَ بِكُمُ الْأَرْضَ فَإِذَا هِيَ تَمُورُ ۝ أَمْ أَمِنتُم مَّن فِي السَّمَاءِ أَن يُرْسِلَ عَلَيْكُمْ حَاصِبًا فَسَتَعْلَمُونَ كَيْفَ نَذِيرِ ۝}$$

Do you feel secure against Him Who is in heaven
causing the earth to swallow you up
when suddenly it rocks from side to side?
Or do you feel secure against Him Who is in heaven
releasing against you a sudden squall of stones,
so that you will know how true My warning was?

Rasul, sallallahu 'alayhi wa sallam, asked, "Where is Allah?" and the girl pointed to heaven and he said that her Iman was correct. In Qur'an Allah says: "Do you feel secure against Him Who is in heaven," which is a way of speaking which indicates the Divine Reality. It goes from the statement to the meaning of it and these two are not disconnected, they are one reality in the intellect of the 'Arif.

Let us go to Surat Ta Ha (20:1-5):

بِسْمِ اللَّهِ الرَّحْمَٰنِ الرَّحِيمِ

طه ۰ مَآ أَنزَلْنَا عَلَيْكَ ٱلْقُرْءَانَ لِتَشْقَىٰٓ ۰ إِلَّا تَذْكِرَةً
لِّمَن يَخْشَىٰ ۰ تَنزِيلًا مِّمَّنْ خَلَقَ ٱلْأَرْضَ وَٱلسَّمَٰوَٰتِ ٱلْعُلَى ۰
ٱلرَّحْمَٰنُ عَلَى ٱلْعَرْشِ ٱسْتَوَىٰ ۰

In the name of Allah, All-Merciful, Most Merciful

Ta Ha
We did not send down the Qur'an to you
to make you miserable

You could also take that as an evidence that Allah did not
send down the Qur'an for people to become Shi'a because it makes them miserable to have to believe all the
terrible things they have to believe in! So:

Ta Ha
We did not send down the Qur'an to you
to make you miserable,
but only as a reminder for those who have fear,
a Revelation from Him Who created
the earth and the high heavens,
the All-Merciful,
established firmly upon the Throne.

Now we go to Surat al-Mujadala (58:7):

اَلَمْ تَرَ أَنَّ اللَّهَ يَعْلَمُ مَا فِي السَّمَوَاتِ وَمَا فِي الْأَرْضِ مَا يَكُونُ مِن نَّجْوَىٰ
ثَلَاثَةٍ إِلَّا هُوَ رَابِعُهُمْ وَلَا خَمْسَةٍ إِلَّا هُوَ سَادِسُهُمْ وَلَا أَدْنَىٰ مِن
ذَٰلِكَ وَلَا أَكْثَرَ إِلَّا هُوَ مَعَهُمْ أَيْنَ مَا كَانُوا ثُمَّ يُنَبِّئُهُم بِمَا عَمِلُوا يَوْمَ
الْقِيَامَةِ إِنَّ اللَّهَ بِكُلِّ شَيْءٍ عَلِيمٌ ۝

Do you not see that Allah knows
what is in the heavens and on the earth?
Three men cannot confer together secretly
without Him being the fourth of them,
or five without Him being the sixth of them,
or fewer than that or more
without Him being with them wherever they are.
Then He will inform them on the Day of Rising
of what they did.
Allah has knowledge of all things.

Again, Allah, subhanahu wa ta'ala, is explaining how He
is with the creatures and He is involving space and time
and presence and number, so that He is one of number –
this is Allah Who is One and nothing can be associated
with Him. Allah says: "Three men cannot confer together secretly without Him being the fourth of them, or
five without Him being the sixth of them, or fewer than
that or more." It is extended to say that whatever number
it is, He is able to take this condition of His knowledge
to be the truth of the matter. Thus place does not prevent
Him being in the place, and number does not prevent
Him adding to that number by His being there, and
Allah has knowledge of all things.

VII

We confirm that Allah, subhanahu wa ta'ala, created times, places, directions, phrases, words, the one who speaks them, and the in-time creatures who are addressed. This is Allah's creation. But the 'Arif knows that when the connective tools of phrase are applied to the Real they have an aspect other than connection or resemblance. So the connection cannot be the affair, and the resemblance cannot be the affair.

There is a group of people who are confronted with these astonishing statements in the Qur'an who neither connect, nor anthropomorphise, nor say, "This is like a man, this is actually how it is," and they do not put one foot into the zone of ta'wil. Ta'wil is when you interpret things saying, "Well, it is in a special way," and you give a kind of secret meaning to it. For example the relationship of the man to the ghost – you cannot use ta'wil to deal with this matter. This group of people do not use ta'wil, they say, "I do not know."

A single sentence – "I do not know," but we avoid letting it be on Him by connection since Allah, subhanahu wa ta'ala, has said in Surat Ash-Shura (42:11):

لَيْسَ كَمِثْلِهِۦ شَىْءٌ

Nothing is like Him.

Faced with this the 'Arif says: "I do not know," because, "Nothing is like Him." The 'Arifin are thus free of ta'wil because they will not make the statement into a hidden meaning, or interpret it in a secret way, and they are free

141

of tatil – the denial of Attributes. They will not deny Attributes of power, that He would act and He would do if He so wanted. This group empty their hearts of thought and speculation and they say: "We have gained in ourselves esteem for the Haqq. May His Majesty be exalted."

Therefore we cannot reach Ma'rifa by fine reflection and investigation. At this point the elite 'Arifin suspect the mutakallimun, the people of teaching and intellect, and they suspect the muhadithun who even produce texts to back up this matter. So they have to move, they have to travel on the path, and this is Tariqa as-Sufiyya.

They have to move otherwise they would be munafiqun, having bad thoughts about the 'ulama! They have to free the heart from logical speculation. They have to sit with Allah in dhikr on what Muhiyuddin Ibn al-'Arabi called the Carpet of Adab, and in muraqaba, watching their own hearts.

Allah takes charge of our instruction by unveiling and Ma'rifa, and so they enter the hal of these ayats we will now look at. Surat al-Anfal (8:29):

$$\text{يَٰٓأَيُّهَا ٱلَّذِينَ ءَامَنُوٓاْ إِن تَتَّقُواْ ٱللَّهَ يَجۡعَل لَّكُمۡ فُرۡقَانًا}$$

You who have Iman! If you have taqwa of Allah,
He will give you discrimination.

In other words, of these ayats, of this Revelation of Allah speaking of Himself in a matter that seems to involve in-timeness, presence, movement and so on, if you who have Iman have taqwa of Allah, awe and fear of Allah, He will give discrimination.

Now we will go to Surat al-Baqara (2:281), at the end of this long ayat:

$$\text{وَاتَّقُوا اللَّهَ وَيُعَلِّمُكُمُ اللَّهُ}$$

Have taqwa of Allah and Allah will give you knowledge.

What is required for knowledge of Allah is not ratiocination, is not reflection, is not philosophy, is not programme – what is necessary is to fear Allah and have taqwa of Allah, to be careful with Allah, and "Allah will give you knowledge." The Arabic is so beautiful – 'yu'allimukum Allah', it is like, 'you will be knowledged'!

These ayats we are looking at are progressive: "Have taqwa of Allah and He will give you discrimination," "Have taqwa of Allah and Allah will give you knowledge," and now Surat Ta Ha (20:114), the very last line of the ayat:

$$\text{وَقُل رَّبِّ زِدْنِي عِلْمًا}$$

And say, 'My Lord, increase me in knowledge.'

"Have taqwa of Allah and Allah will give you knowledge." Now you reach that point where you become active and you say, "My Lord, increase me in knowledge." Give it to me! This is another step. You are able to ask for it, you have not become passive, and this is what is called in the language of Tasawwuf, himma. You want this thing, you are demanding it, you are insisting on it.

$$ رَّبِّ زِدْنِي عِلْمًا ۝ $$

My Lord, increase me in knowledge.

This is the active tense. This is the man moving into knowledge, and entering the hal of this ayat is your du'a to Allah, subhanahu wa ta'ala.

We finish with Surat al-Kahf (18:65):

$$ فَوَجَدَا عَبْدًا مِّنْ عِبَادِنَآ ءَاتَيْنَاهُ رَحْمَةً مِّنْ عِندِنَا وَعَلَّمْنَاهُ مِن لَّدُنَّا عِلْمًا ۝ $$

They found a slave of Ours
whom We had granted mercy from Us
and whom We had also given knowledge direct from Us.

This is to say that the mercy which was granted to the slave was the Khatm of the destiny. Allah had decreed that this person would be 'Arif because it is not by your choosing, it is by His choosing because He is the Doer. The first thing you have to understand for this man to be this man:

$$ رَحْمَةً مِّنْ عِندِنَا $$

mercy from Us

– the mercy that Allah gave to the slave was a good seal on his destiny. He destined him for this knowledge. That is why the du'a of the mumin is, "O Allah, give me an Iman that is lasting," because you want your Iman to continue throughout your life so that, like the wine in the bottle, it becomes richer although nothing more enters the bottle. The bottle remains, and what is in it slowly changes its quality becoming stronger and richer. This is the Khatm of the destiny.

The second part of the ayat is:

$$وَعَلَّمْنَاهُ مِن لَّدُنَّا عِلْمًا ۝$$

And whom We had also given knowledge direct from Us.

This is the path of the people who have this pure Tanzih of associating nothing with Allah. Surat Ash-Shura (42:11):

$$لَيْسَ كَمِثْلِهِ شَيْءٌ$$

Nothing is like Him, as we mentioned from Qur'an earlier. With this you come out of the circle of the people who say, "If He says, 'He sat on the Throne' then He sat on the Throne," which is ignorance. And you come out from the philosophers' position who say, "It is a metaphor. It is as if He sat on the Throne but He did not really sit on the Throne."

We take the Arabic language and say No. The joined phrase makes us see that this tells us that. There is no metaphor. There is structurally no such thing in Arabic grammar as a simile, it is the joined phrase. Thus if it says this, it is this. It is both of these things. The philosophers say, "You must not say that He sat on the Throne because that would be to connect Him to forms, so it is a metaphor and it is not real." But it is neither of these things.

The pure Tanzih is that it cannot be approached in this way. Imam Malik, radiyallahu 'anhu, said, "The sitting on the Throne is known. The way is not known, and to question it is bida'." In other words, it is something the understanding of which can only be arrived at on the Carpet of Adab in dhikr and in muraqaba. Then Allah will unveil for you these states, and then Allah, subhanahu wa ta'ala, will say to you: "Draw near."

HADRA

We ask Allah, subhanahu wa ta'ala, to confound all the enemies of Islam. We ask Allah, subhanahu wa ta'ala, by the baraka that He has given to the Du'a an-Nasiri that within all our hearts it should be answered by the angels in following the supplications in it.

We ask Allah, subhanahu wa ta'ala, to confound and confuse the enemies of Islam. We ask Allah, subhanahu wa ta'ala, to scatter the remnants of christianity, judaism and buddhism and all the false religions on the earth. We ask Allah, subhanahu wa ta'ala, to raise up and exalt Islam above what the Arabs have done to it. We ask Allah, subhanahu wa ta'ala, to let the Arabs return to Islam by Your Mercy.

VII

We ask Allah, subhanahu wa ta'ala, to establish the Deen all over the land of India and we ask Allah, subhanahu wa ta'ala, to confound its enemies. We ask Allah, subhanahu wa ta'ala, to give victory to the Muslims. We ask Allah, subhanahu wa ta'ala, to give the leadership of the Muslims from among the community of the dhakirun.

VIII

MAY 22ND 2004

Each week we have been pursuing a path to gaining a stronger and deeper knowledge of Tawhid. We have emphasised through all this that there is a dimension of this knowledge which is in itself the reality of your fear of Allah, subhanahu wa ta'ala. "Fear Allah and He will give you knowledge."

It is very important that you remember during all of this that this is something to be approached by reflection and by inwardly achieving states and arriving at certain stations. There is the fulfilment of the true knowledge of Tawhid which is, in the language of the Sufis, the 'Tajrid of Tawhid'. This is the stripping away of your consciousness of self before the Presence of Allah, subhanahu wa ta'ala.

We are now going to look at something which may seem a little complicated but it is not. Be patient, and just let the first stage of it flow over you, so to speak. We are going to look at a technical framework, and you must understand that we are now speaking as Muslims sitting in the mosque, talking about Allah, subhanahu wa ta'ala, and there is not anything in this that is similar to the way we talk about objects and things in the world.

We are trying to get at an understanding of Tawhid which also has in it this adab without which there is no path to this understanding. It is edged in with all kinds of conditions and inhibitions to prevent you having a wrong kind of thinking about Allah, subhanahu wa ta'ala, because these are the deviations and the things which anger Allah that are referred to in the Fatiha.

We are going to look at something in this technical language which you must all know, because you must go into the world with a secure Tawhid which cannot be shaken and which cannot be swept away by modern innovations, or by philosophy. It is not the proper business of philosophy. This term is called 'Tanazzulat'. Tanazzulat is like the unfolding descent from the Essence of Allah, subhanahu wa ta'ala, into the process by which He makes the creation. Again, bear in mind the detailed care with which we have confirmed that Allah is exalted above anything associated with Him and that He is not connected to anything, He is not dependent on anything, He has not come from anything and no thing has come out from Him.

We are going to describe the amazing process which results in our being here and results in the enormous vast creation of the universe of which He is the sole Creator, and exalted above it. We could say that it is something in reality but the description does not fit it, or it is something in description and this does not attain to the reality of it.

This descent is called the Tanazzulat as-Sita, the six-staged descent or unfolding of these stages by which we are able to understand the amazing reality of Allah, Creator of the universe. Shaykh Muhiyuddin Ibn al-'Arabi said: "You are not going to understand Allah, but you may reflect on the universe." It is by your reflection on the universe that you understand the majesty and power of Allah, subhanahu wa ta'ala.

This unfolding of the power and majesty of Allah, subhanahu wa ta'ala, is divided into six. Three of these ranks are utterly to do with Allah, and the other three are to do with how Allah manifests in the creation, the things to do with the world. The first are the 'Murati billahi', the Divine Ranks, which are three. Ahadiyat, Wahdat and Wahidiyat. These terms, which sound very forbidding to begin with, are all part of the enormous adab of those men who have been given the gift of unveiling by Allah, subhanahu wa ta'ala, who have come back from that illumination to speak about Allah in a way which fills us with awe and increases our fear of Allah, subhanahu wa ta'ala.

The first stage is Ahadiyat. This represents the Essence. The Essence is pure, disconnected from all forms and indeterminate. It is Allah in His unique Oneness, with nothing associated with Him, and with vast and tremendous powers hidden in this Oneness. It is also called the 'Mist' because someone asked the Rasul, sallallahu 'alayhi wa sallam: "Where was Allah before the creation of the world?" which is not a correct question, but Rasul, sallallahu 'alayhi wa sallam, said, "He was in the 'Amma', the Mist." In other words, it is unknowable. This is a term which we will come to in more detail in a moment.

So Ahadiyat is the Essence. Wahdat is the Unity. These are all ways of speaking about Allah, subhanahu wa ta'ala. We have not yet looked at the manifestation of the creation. The third term is Wahidiyat which is Unity which has in it the knowledge of plurality – Allah's knowledge that there can be the many myriad things.

The worldly ranks are called the Murati bil-Kawni, the ranks of the created forms. These are three: Ruh – which is the spirit, Mithal – which is the likenesses, the metaphoric capacity for form to take place, and Jism which is the body itself. These are the six ranks and then below this comes Insan, man.

We are going to look at this in detail. After Ahadiyat which is Essence, you have from Wahdat to Wahidiyat manifestation, not yet in the creation, but in Allah's, subhanahu wa ta'ala, knowledge of these potentials of His own majesty. From the ruh to the mithal, to the jism to the insan – the spirit to the likenesses, to the body to man – these are the external manifestations. These are when this enormous majestic power of Allah unfolds itself in the creation of the forms.

We will look at Ahadiyat. Ahadiyat is the absolute Being of Allah, unknown and unknowable. It is what Rasul, sallallahu 'alayhi wa sallam, warned people not to contemplate because it could destroy them, because it is not possible. Sayyiduna Abu Bakr as-Siddiq, radiyallahu 'anhu, made the famous statement on it which is used and referred to by all the Sufis and considered the final statement about it: "Your incapacity to know is all that you can know." Shaykh Ibn al-'Arabi said that this tremendous statement was not a negative statement, it was illumination. To know that you do not know is a kind of knowing. This is the adab on which this matter is dealt with.

The great Sufi, Jili said: "The Essence means the absolute dropping of all modes, all adjuncts, all relations, all aspects." In other words, it is the Creator before one talks of Him as the Creator. It is the Almighty in His Essence, the Dhat of Allah which in Qur'an is the Wajh, the Face, face being the indicator of the essence of the person.

We will look at Surat Al 'Imran (3:28 and 30), which we have looked at before and which we have to look at again in order that we are correct in our adab about understanding the Essence of Allah, subhanahu wa ta'ala, and which defines the understanding we have of Allah:

$$ وَيُحَذِّرُكُمُ اللَّهُ نَفْسَهُ $$

Allah advises you to be afraid of Him.

This is the Qur'anic injunction which contains the same

message. The being afraid of Allah and the being aware of Him – you cannot go beyond this understanding of Him, you cannot contemplate the Essence, you cannot understand the Essence and you cannot know the Essence. At this point He is hidden, He is unknown, unknowable, all His power is hidden. It is the unattainable absolute which is the Ahad of Allah, subhanahu wa ta'ala.

The Sufis have given this different names because they are so anxious that it has to be preserved before they contemplate the astonishing reality which is His creation. The Sufis have called this the Ghayb al-Ghuyub – the Unseen of the Unseen, and they have called it the 'Ayn al-Mutlaq – Absolute Essence. A very beautiful name the Sufis of the East have given it, which is in Hujwiri, is 'Aynal-Kafur – the Source of Camphor. Whatever enters into camphor becomes camphor, it has not any otherness. This is a beautiful and poetic expression for this absolute nature of Allah. That is the first stage of this Tanazzulat.

The second stage is Wahdat. The 'Arif recognises that Allah is One, knows Himself, is aware of all His potentialities and that He alone exists and has the power of manifestation. This is the first determination. The Sufis name it Al-Haqiqat al-Muhammadiya. We will look into this and find that this is a pure statement and does not contain any wrong thinking, but has to be understood.

So this second unfolding of Allah's power that we are able to understand is called Wahdat, Unity. These are pure potentialities of the Essence without any implied multiplicity. We are not talking yet about multiplicity, about creation, we are still within an understanding of the Divine Reality. We recognise four aspects: Wujud – which is existence, 'Ilm – which is knowledge, Nur – which is light, and Shuhud – which is witnessing.

Then we are able to say: Allah exists, knows His Being, His Attributes and His Actions. He is self-revealing and self-manifest. He witnesses His own Being, because the knowledge is in His witnessing of His own Being. All this is Essence itself. Identical with it, it does not proceed from the Essence and it is not prior to the Essence, thus it is Essence. Therefore Essence itself is Existence, Existent, and conscious of its existence. Essence itself is Knowledge, the Knower and the Known. Essence itself is the Light, the Lighter and the Lighted, and is itself Observance, Observer and Observed. We are still not talking about the creation but about how Allah is.

This stage of our understanding of Allah's Essence, in fact, contains all the Attributes of the Divine and the worldly Names, and all the created things destined for the creation, as the whole is included in the inwardness of the Essence. The knowledge of it, the existence of it, the light – and by that light that it is self-observing. The metaphor of this is that the whole date tree is hidden in the date stone – it is not there, but the whole tree is there.

The Sufis name this Tajalli al-Awwal – the first manifestation. It is the first emergence, as it were, for us to have a sort of knowledge about Allah, subhanahu wa ta'ala. They call it Wujud al-Awwal, the first existence.

Jawhar al-Awwal – the first jewel form. But the great Sufis have named this station of the speaking about Allah, subhanahu wa ta'ala, "Al-Haqiqat al-Muhammadiya."

This is because the human manifestation is above that of the things in the creation. So he, sallallahu 'alayhi wa sallam, is the highest manifestation among men. Follow this carefully to the end because it could look like something that we cannot accept, and this is not possible. Rasul, sallallahu 'alayhi wa sallam, said, "I am the first of the sons of Adam," and we also have that he is the last of the Messengers, he is the Seal of the Messengers.

To understand this the Sufis say that the materialists say that the function of the fruit is to produce the tree. But the 'Arifin say that the reality of the tree is that it is the fruit which is intended. Rasul, sallallahu 'alayhi wa sallam, is intended with the whole creation because he is the perfect manifestation of man in his being the first of the ones who praise Allah, and he recognises His Attributes and His Power and is able to bear the Message that is sent to him from Allah, subhanahu wa ta'ala.

We have to understand that the dhat, the essence of Muhammad, is not the Haqiqat al-Muhammadiya. The Haqiqat al-Muhammadiya belongs to the Knower and Allah is the Knower. The dhat of the Messenger is what is known. The 'abd is not the Rabb, the slave is not the Lord. His dhat is that of the slave, but his Haqiqat, his reality is with Allah. There is no association.

So what is called the Haqiqat al-Muhammadiya is not

the essence of the Rasul, sallallahu 'alayhi wa sallam,
because this would be shirk and it would be kufr.

We go to Surat al-Ma'ida (85:17 and 18). This explains
exactly what we mean:

$$\text{لَقَدْ كَفَرَ ٱلَّذِينَ قَالُوٓا۟}$$

$$\text{إِنَّ ٱللَّهَ هُوَ ٱلْمَسِيحُ ٱبْنُ}$$

$$\text{مَرْيَمَ قُلْ فَمَن يَمْلِكُ مِنَ ٱللَّهِ شَيْئًا إِنْ أَرَادَ أَنْ}$$

$$\text{يُهْلِكَ ٱلْمَسِيحَ ٱبْنَ مَرْيَمَ وَأُمَّهُ وَمَن فِى ٱلْأَرْضِ}$$

$$\text{جَمِيعًا وَلِلَّهِ مُلْكُ ٱلسَّمَٰوَٰتِ وَٱلْأَرْضِ وَمَا بَيْنَهُمَا}$$

$$\text{يَخْلُقُ مَا يَشَآءُ وَٱللَّهُ عَلَىٰ كُلِّ شَىْءٍ قَدِيرٌ ۝}$$

$$\text{وَقَالَتِ ٱلْيَهُودُ وَٱلنَّصَٰرَىٰ نَحْنُ أَبْنَٰٓؤُا۟ ٱللَّهِ وَأَحِبَّٰٓؤُهُۥ قُلْ}$$

$$\text{فَلِمَ يُعَذِّبُكُم بِذُنُوبِكُم بَلْ أَنتُم بَشَرٌ مِّمَّنْ خَلَقَ يَغْفِرُ لِمَن}$$

$$\text{يَشَآءُ وَيُعَذِّبُ مَن يَشَآءُ وَلِلَّهِ مُلْكُ ٱلسَّمَٰوَٰتِ وَٱلْأَرْضِ}$$

$$\text{وَمَا بَيْنَهُمَا وَإِلَيْهِ ٱلْمَصِيرُ ۝}$$

Those who say, 'Allah is the Messiah,
son of Maryam,' are kafir.
Say: 'Who possesses any power at all over Allah
if He desires to destroy the Messiah, son of Maryam,
and his mother, and everyone else on earth?'
The kingdom of the heavens and the earth
and everything between them

belongs to Allah.
He creates whatever He wills.
Allah has power over all things.

The jews and christians say,
'We are Allah's children and His loved ones.'
Say: 'Why, then, does He punish you
for your wrong actions?
No, you are merely human beings
among those He has created.
He forgives whomever He wills
and He punishes whomever He wills.
The kingdom of the heavens and the earth
and everything between them belongs to Allah.
He is our final destination.'

Here we have the explanation of how what is being said does not have any shred or implication of identification, of joining or linkage, of connection between the presence of Rasul, sallallahu 'alayhi wa sallam, and the Essence and the Reality of Allah, subhanahu wa ta'ala.

"Those who say, 'Allah is the Messiah, son of Maryam,' are kafir." So much for all these calls for the Muslims to have 'dialogue' with the christians! All we need to do is to put that in an envelope and send it to them.

لَقَدْ كَفَرَ ٱلَّذِينَ قَالُوٓاْ
إِنَّ ٱللَّهَ هُوَٱلْمَسِيحُ ٱبْنُ مَرْيَمَ

VIII

Those who say, 'Allah is the Messiah,
son of Maryam,' are kafir.

These are Allah's words.

قُل فَمَن يَمْلِكُ مِنَ ٱللَّهِ شَيْئًا إِنْ أَرَادَ أَن
يُهْلِكَ ٱلْمَسِيحَ ٱبْنَ مَرْيَمَ وَأُمَّهُ وَمَن فِى ٱلْأَرْضِ
جَمِيعًا وَلِلَّهِ مُلْكُ ٱلسَّمَٰوَٰتِ وَٱلْأَرْضِ وَمَا بَيْنَهُمَا
يَخْلُقُ مَا يَشَآءُ وَٱللَّهُ عَلَىٰ كُلِّ شَىْءٍ قَدِيرٌ ۝
وَقَالَتِ ٱلْيَهُودُ وَٱلنَّصَٰرَىٰ نَحْنُ أَبْنَٰٓؤُاْ ٱللَّهِ وَأَحِبَّٰٓؤُهُۥ قُلْ
فَلِمَ يُعَذِّبُكُم بِذُنُوبِكُم بَلْ أَنتُم بَشَرٌ مِّمَّنْ خَلَقَ يَغْفِرُ لِمَن
يَشَآءُ وَيُعَذِّبُ مَن يَشَآءُ وَلِلَّهِ مُلْكُ ٱلسَّمَٰوَٰتِ وَٱلْأَرْضِ
وَمَا بَيْنَهُمَا وَإِلَيْهِ ٱلْمَصِيرُ ۝

Say: 'Who possesses any power at all over Allah
if He desires to destroy the Messiah, son of Maryam,
and his mother, and everyone else on earth?'
The kingdom of the heavens and the earth
and everything between them belongs to Allah.
He creates whatever He wills.
Allah has power over all things.

The jews and christians say,
'We are Allah's children and His loved ones.'
Say: 'Why, then, does He punish you
for your wrong actions?

159

No, you are merely human beings
among those He has created.
He forgives whomever He wills
and He punishes whomever He wills.
The kingdom of the heavens and the earth
and everything between them belongs to Allah.
He is our final destination.'

Sometimes this stage of unfolding of Allah's majesty and power is called Nuri Muhammadi. If we look at the Diwan of Shaykh Muhammad ibn al-Habib, radiyallahu 'anhu, and the Wird which we have just recited:

اَللَّهُمَّ صَلِّ وَسَلِّم بِأَنْوَاعٍ كَمَالَاتِكَ فِي جَمِيعِ تَجَلِّيَاتِكَ عَلَى سَيِّدِنَا وَ

مَوْلَانَا مُحَمَّدٍ أَوَّلِ الْأَنْوَارِ الْفَائِضَةِ مِنْ بُحُورِ عَظَمَةِ الذَّاتِ

"The first of the lights emanating from the oceans of the sublimity of the Essence." That is a reference to the Nuri Muhammad, the Haqiqat al-Muhammadiya. It is very important for the one who takes the journey of Ma'rifa to understand this aspect of the Divinity.

We will see later when we look at the Diwan where Shaykh Muhammad ibn al-Habib, radiyallahu 'anhu, gives his definition of Tawhid and defines how part of Tawhid is contained in proper knowledge of Rasul, sal-lallahu 'alayhi wa sallam. Again, this is not in any way to deify him yet to recognise his high spiritual place. Remember the very important thing which Mawlana Rumi said about Abu Jahl: when he looked he did not see the Rasul but the son of 'Abdullah. There is a spiritual rank which is not the property of Rasul, sallallahu 'alayhi wa sallam, but that a light has been put into him which gives him the rank so that he said, "I am the first of the sons of Adam." He does not say that he is not one of the sons of Adam. Allah, subhanahu wa ta'ala, reminds us in Surat Al 'Imran, referring to the Prophet's future death (3:144-145):

$$\text{وَمَا مُحَمَّدٌ اِلَّا رَسُولٌ}$$

$$\text{قَدْ خَلَتْ مِن قَبْلِهِ الرُّسُلُ اَفَاِيْن مَاتَ اَوْقُتِلَ اَنقَلَبْتُمْ}$$

$$\text{عَلَى اَعْقَابِكُمْ وَمَنْ يَنقَلِبْ عَلَى عَقِبَيْهِ فَلَنْ يَّضُرَّ اللَّهَ شَيْئًا}$$

$$\text{وَسَيَجْزِے اللَّهُ الشَّاكِرِيْنَ ۝ وَمَاكَانَ لِنَفْسٍ اَن}$$

$$\text{تَمُوتَ اِلَّا بِاِذْنِ اللَّهِ كِتَابًا مُّؤَجَّلًا}$$

Muhammad is only a Messenger
and he has been preceded by other Messengers.
If he were to die or be killed,
would you turn on your heels?
Those who turn on their heels
do not harm Allah in any way.
Allah will recompense the thankful.
No self can die except with Allah's permission,
at a predetermined time.

So Allah's confirmation of this is the absolute impossibility for the Muslims to think about Rasul, sallallahu 'alayhi wa sallam, in that way. At the same time, in this

modern age, we have had a denigration of Rasul, sallallahu 'alayhi wa sallam, and a bringing-down from his
high position as the first of the sons of Adam and the
Seal of the Messengers – by Egyptian scholars and the
shayateen from Arabia who have been like Abu Jahl and
have tried to say that he is merely the son of his father.

Without any shirk, without any kufr and without any
crossing of this line that we will never, never cross, you
have to recognise the high position which the Rasul,
sallallahu 'alayhi wa sallam, has and the high position he
has been given by Allah, subhanahu wa ta'ala, in the ayat
of the Salat an-Nabiy (Surat al-Ahzab 56):

إِنَّ ٱللَّهَ وَمَلَٰٓئِكَتَهُۥ يُصَلُّونَ عَلَى ٱلنَّبِىِّ
يَٰٓأَيُّهَا ٱلَّذِينَ ءَامَنُوا۟ صَلُّوا۟ عَلَيْهِ وَسَلِّمُوا۟ تَسْلِيمًا ۝

Allah and His angels call down blessings on the Prophet.
You who have Iman! call down blessings on him
and ask for complete peace and safety for him.

To go back to this confirmation of Allah being exalted
above everything, every form and every human being,
Dhun-Nun al-Misri speaks of the Essence in this way:

علم ذات الحق جهل
تعريف حق المعرفة حيرة
إشارة المشير شرك

Knowledge of the Essence of the Haqq – ignorance.
Definition of the reality of Ma'rifa – bewilderment.
Indication by an indicator – shirk.

You cannot even make an ishara on this matter! Shirk.
The line is drawn and the mouths are silent.

The poets of the Sufis use the Anqa', which is a mytho-
logical bird, to speak about the Essence, and one of them
said, "Do not try to catch the Anqa', you will only be
able to catch air." This is the knowledge of the Essence
of Allah, subhanahu wa ta'ala. Inshallah we will continue
with these six terms having done the first two of the
three Divine ranks. Then we will move to the three
worldly ranks, inshallah.

IX

May 29th 2004

We have been looking at the 'Tanazzulat as-Sita'. These stages are not in time or preceding the other, or following the other, but they are only in description. They are understood in their detail by the 'Arifin and they are also understood by the mutakallimun because they follow in a logical pattern what one may say about Allah, subhanahu wa ta'ala, with correct adab.

This Tanazzulat as-Sita is divided into three Murati billahi, Divine ranks, and then the next three are the Murati bil-Kawni, the worldly ranks. In other words, the first three are what you can say about Allah, subhanahu wa ta'ala – their different aspects of Essence. We talked about Ahadiyat which is Essence – pure, disconnected from any forms and indeterminate, having no specificity of any kind. Then we came on Wahdat, which is unity and it is between Ahadiyat and Wahidiyat.

Wahdat is called in the language of the Sufis, Nuri Muhammadi, and is more generally called the Haqiqat al-Muhammadiya. Remember that we pointed out that this is not the essence of the Messenger, sallallahu 'alayhi wa sallam, which is different from his Haqiqat because the Messenger is a human being and cannot be associated in any way with the Divine as he is ordered to explain in the Qur'an itself.

Another name of this is the Tajalli al-Awwal, the first manifestation. Or Wujudi al-Awwal, the first existence, or the Jawhar al-Awwal, the first jewel. All this is within the Essence of Allah, subhanahu wa ta'ala.

After Wahdat, which is like a barzakh between Ahadiyat and Wahidiyat, we come to Wahidiyat. When the 'Arif reflects on the Dhat of Allah, of Allah possessing knowledge in detail – its Names, Attributes and source-forms with all the distinctions and aspects – this is called Wahidiyat. Now we can talk about Allah, subhanahu wa ta'ala, as possessing knowledge in detail in Himself, and His Names and Attributes and source-forms of all those knowledges which allow all the myriad forms in the universe to unfold and become manifest on the command of the 'Kun'. This is called Wahidiyat. So Ahadiyat is absoluteness in itself, and Wahidiyat is that with all its details.

Ahadiyat is absolute, Wahdat is implicit – that is why it is
called the barzakh al-Kubra, the great divide in how we
can understand Allah, subhanahu wa ta'ala, and Wahidiyat
is explicit. It is Allah in His supremacy with all His Attributes and Names known to Himself and all His knowledge by which He will unfold, as He desires, the whole
vast creation of the universe. These are three Divine
Names but they are suppositional names, they are not actual, they have no reality – they are for us to understand.

Ahadiyat, Dhat, Essence without conditions. Ahadiyat is
Surat al-Ikhlas:

بِسْمِ اللهِ الرَّحْمَنِ الرَّحِيمِ
قُلْ هُوَ اللَّهُ أَحَدٌ ۝ اللَّهُ الصَّمَدُ ۝ لَمْ يَلِدْ
وَلَمْ يُولَدْ ۝ وَلَمْ يَكُن لَّهُ كُفُوًا أَحَدٌ ۝

In the name of Allah, All-Merciful, Most Merciful
"Say: 'He is Allah, Absolute Oneness,
Allah, the Everlasting Sustainer of all.
He has not given birth and was not born.
And no one is comparable to Him.'"

The Ahad is Ahadiyat. Secondly Wahdat, the barzakh.
This is unity but with potentiality. It is potential to have
this vast unfolding of forms but still not determined, it is
still not specified what Allah's unfolding will be.

Thirdly Wahidiyat, we would call the emergence of the
Names. All this is within Allah's Divine Reality, not in the

universe, not in the world of forms. It is the potential of His majesty – the emergence of the Names and the Attributes and what we called earlier the 'ayan ath-thabita, the source-forms. In other words, the form of the creature is in the knowledge of Allah, or the thing as He wishes it to be, before it is realised. Metaphorically it is the potter with the image of the pot before the pot is thrown, but there is no connection and the metaphor cannot be extended because Allah has no outsideness or insideness, or nearness or farness from His objects. Yet it is a metaphor of how the forms have to exist in His knowledge before they manifest and become the known to us.

For this we look at Surat al-Baqara (2:163):

وَإِلَٰهُكُمْ إِلَٰهٌ وَاحِدٌ لَّا إِلَٰهَ إِلَّا هُوَ ٱلرَّحْمَٰنُ ٱلرَّحِيمُ ۝

Your God is One God. There is no god but Him, the All-Merciful, the Most Merciful.

Now we have the Ahad unfolding His Attributes. "Your God is One God. There is no god but Him," nothing is associated with Him so He is not connected to the world of forms, He is not connected to His creation in any way whatsoever. He is exalted above it, and He is "the All-Merciful, the Most Merciful." He has Rahman and He has Rahim. These are His Attributes, these are His qualities, this is Him showing Himself for what He is as the Lord of the Universe.

وَإِلَٰهُكُمْ إِلَٰهٌ وَاحِدٌ لَّا إِلَٰهَ إِلَّا هُوَ ٱلرَّحْمَٰنُ ٱلرَّحِيمُ ۝

Here we have Essence and Attributes. Allah is One. This is the Ahadiyat which we have been looking at. "There is no god but Him," so the Wahdat, which we have said is everything in potential and is the Nuri Muhammad, still does not allow anything in that stage to be connected to Him. "The All-Merciful, the Most Merciful." Then He shows the splendour of His Attributes and the two dominant Attributes of His qualities are the Rahman and the Rahim which is why of course all but one of the surats of Qur'an begins with: "Bismillahi ar-Rahmani ar-Rahim." Bismillah – in the name of Allah, the Ahad, and the Rahman and the Rahim. In other words Qur'an puts Allah's Unity with His Attributes throughout.

This does not mean that there was Absolute which then became latent with powers and potentials and then became Existent. You must understand this because we are not saying that. This is a description for your clarity, and it is confirmed by the 'Arifin in their vision and their knowledge. It is a description which has not got time in it. It is not that He was this and then He was that. He is One, immutable and unchangeable always.

Rasul, sallallahu 'alayhi wa sallam, was asked, "Where was Allah before the creation?" and he replied, "Before the creation of the world, Allah was and there was nothing with Him." Imam Junayd confirmed this and made commentary on it by saying, "Is as He was."

The Names indicate the Essence along with its Attributes. In other words, when you are given the Attribute ar-Rahman, this is Allah, this is the Essence manifesting

Attribute. You cannot have the Attribute without the Essence so: Allahu Ahad, Allahu Samad. The Essence goes with the Name.

Shaykh al-Akbar tells of a Wali who was asked how he achieved his Ma'rifa and he replied, "By joining the opposite Attributes. The One Who Exalts and the One Who Brings Low." Also, Al-Awwalu wal-Akhiru, wadh-Dhahiru wal-Batin. So he joined these opposites because they are One, Allah is One, until he achieved his fana'.

With Wahidiyat emerge the four mother Attributes and they are: Hayy, 'Ilm, Irada and Qudra – life, knowledge, will and power. From these come all the Attributes of the hearing, the seeing and so on. From Allah as Al-'Alim comes the knowledge of the source-forms, the 'ayan ath-thabita. He knows that from this is the knowledge by which He knows how all the things will have form. Remember that we are saying that Allah is One in His Essence and in His Attributes and in His Acts because the form is not a static thing. Everything in the creation is alive. According to the Sufis, all the apparently inanimate things are also alive. This was something that they said from the time of Rasul, sallallahu 'alayhi wa sallam, but it was only confirmed by the scientists with nuclear science. The apparently dead matter was in fact moving enormously fast and was in motion and alive. This has always been the position of people of vision in Tasawwuf.

So from Al-'Alim comes the knowledge of the source-form. What we are saying is that the source-form is not a form in a static sense because for a living creature you cannot separate its form from its actions. The obvious example is a dog. The dog is not just a creature with four legs and a tail and a head – the essence of dog is that he hunts, he attaches to man and is loyal to man, he can turn on man, he is a guard, he is not clean – that is dog. So dog cannot be separated from dogness. Just as that is the case, so when we come to man. Allah creates the form of the man and also the history of the man, thus the whole man from the beginning of his coming into existence in the world until his death has been created by Allah, subhanahu wa ta'ala. Thus he will behave according to his form, he has no choice.

What the ignorant people call freedom is not what we understand by freedom. What we understand by complete freedom is complete 'ubudiyya, complete slavehood, because if you are completely the slave of Allah, subhanahu wa ta'ala, then you are liberated because you will move by Him, you will speak by Him, and so your actions will be by Him and pleasing to Him.

Shaykh Ibn al-'Arabi said about these source-forms, the 'ayan ath-thabita: "They never smell the odour of existence." You must understand that the forms on which things come into being have not got any existence. They are in the knowledge of Allah, subhanahu wa ta'ala. Then by the Command, 'Kun', He brings them into existence where they are not the 'ayan ath-thabita but the forms themselves. These 'ayan ath-thabita have no external existence, they are only subsistent in Knowledge. Every essence of a thing has a distinguishing nature or characteristic to distinguish it from other apparently similar forms.

In other words, each being is made on a particular form. That is why all of us are of the same genus but every single one of us is completely different. The finger-print is different, the hand-print is different, the eye – everything of each person is made on that particular form of Allah's Command. Thus the Attributes of Al-'Alim have endless possibilities. This is the form of the created beings, and we look for this in Surat al-Isra (17:84). This is a command on the Rasul, sallallahu 'alayhi wa sallam, therefore it is a direct education of the muminun:

$$قُلْ كُلٌّ يَعْمَلُ عَلَىٰ شَاكِلَتِهِ$$

The translation is, "Say: 'Each man acts according to his nature," but I am not satisfied with the translation of 'nature' because actually 'shakilat' is the 'form', the thing we have been talking about. So each man acts according to his 'ayn ath-thabita, to this form he had in the knowledge of Allah, subhanahu wa ta'ala, before he was ordered into existence by the Divine Command that brings things to life. And then:

$$فَرَبُّكُمْ أَعْلَمُ$$

But your Lord knows best –

So here Allah, subhanahu wa ta'ala, speaks of Himself using the term Rabb. Very often in the Qur'an when the term Rabb is used, it is indicating Allah in His capacity, in that aspect of His Essence which manifests through the Attributes to make things happen in the world of forms in the created universe.

$$\text{فَرَبُّكُمْ أَعْلَمُ بِمَنْ هُوَ أَهْدَىٰ سَبِيلًا ۝}$$

But your Lord knows best who is best guided on the path.

Allah knows best who is best guided on the path because the man has been made in that form that will put him on the path. This takes you to the wall of knowledge about the seal of the destiny. You cannot go beyond that knowledge because it is a knowledge that brings you to a complete halt. In other words, when you, by your choices, decide from inside the form that you have to do what you do, it reveals at that moment that Allah has chosen you to be mumin. Therefore you both choose to be mumin but also Allah, subhanahu wa ta'ala, because of His fore-knowledge and because of the nature of His design, had designed you to be mumin.

Beyond that you cannot go because your responsibility is not taken away. If you did not have a responsibility for the acts there would not have been the need for Prophets, for Qur'an, for the Books. You have an absolute responsibility before Allah for the destiny, and at the same time you are in fact acting out what He has designed you for.

What knowledge is, what wisdom is, is that the mumin wants to do what is pleasing to Allah because if He does what is pleasing to Allah it is because Allah has destined him to be one of those people who is pleasing to Him.

When you do act in a way that is pleasing to Allah you are not claiming, "I have done this, look! I have done what is pleasing to Allah," but, "He has put me on this path." The shakilat takes us to this knowledge.

The Tanazzulat then descends into its three worldly ranks which are ruh, mithal and jism. These in turn, in description only, take us to insan, to man. Again, these descents are not in space or time but are a way of understanding this incredible unfolding of the Divine Reality. In terms of the creation, when these Attributes have ordered into being the universe, and when the Throne of Allah has been set out in all its splendour, and the heavens have been created, and then the creatures have been created and the Khalif of Allah, subhanahu wa ta'ala, has been appointed, which is man, then you have ruh, mithal and jism. This is the spirit, mithal and body.

Mithal is that because certain things are like certain things you are able to understand these spiritual matters. You cannot understand them by reason, you cannot understand them except by glimpsing the likeness: "This is like that." You cannot say, "It is that," then, "Ah, you mean so and so," as if it were a real example. A mithal is not an example but a picture of something that makes it clear for you. This is a necessary dimension of the worldly condition.

If you are not able to interpret mithal then it is as though you are not a complete human being. To give you an example: in the medical profession, the psychiatrists' test that someone is insane, therefore not a full human being,

is that they ask them a question like, "What does it mean
if 'people in glass-houses should not throw stones'?" If
the answer is, "Well, if you are in a glass house and you
throw a stone you will break the window," then he is
mad. If he is able to say, "It means you should not accuse
the other when you are in the same situation," that
means he understands the mithal.

If you cannot translate the mithal it is a sign of insanity
because normal reason is actually based on something
that is not reasonable, but is a faculty of the imagination
to understand the situation the human being is in.

I will now take this exactly from Shaykh Muhiyuddin
Ibn al-'Arabi's 'Fusus al-Hikam', 'The Seals of Wisdom',
because it is so clear and so beautiful. He explains the
position of man in the universe:

> "When Allah, subhanahu wa ta'ala, willed (He is
> using His Attribute of Will which is one of the
> Mother Attributes) that the source of His most
> beautiful Names, which are beyond enumer-
> ation, be seen, or you can equally say that He
> willed His source to be seen,"

– because if He wished that the source of His Attributes
be seen, as the Attributes and the Essence are one, it
meant that He wanted somehow to declare out His own
Essence –

> "He willed that they be seen in a microcosmic
> being which contained the entire Command,

175

having been endowed with existence, and through which His secret was manifested to Him."

He willed that the source of His most beautiful Names
be seen in a microcosmic being which contained the
entire Command, the entire universe, because every
aspect of the universe is in man. Man is the microcosm
of the macrocosm. He is the focal point of the whole
thing, he is the end result, he is what is intended by the
creation.

> "He willed that they be seen in a microcosmic
> being which contained the entire command,
> having been endowed with existence, and thr-
> ough which His secret was manifested to Him,"
> for His delight. "For the vision that a thing has
> of itself through itself is not like a vision of itself
> in something else which acts like a mirror for it,
> so He manifests Himself to Himself in a form
> which is bestowed by the place in which He is
> seen. He would not appear thus without the
> existence of this place and His Tajalli to Himself
> in it.

> "Allah brought the entire universe into existence
> with the existence of a form fashioned without
> ruh, like an unpolished mirror. It is a matter of
> the Divine decree that He does not fashion a
> place but that it must receive the Divine ruh
> which is described as being 'blown into it' in
> Qur'an. This is none other than the obtaining of
> the predisposition of that fashioned form to re-

ceive the overflowing, the perpetual Tajalli which has never ceased and which will never cease."

So he is saying that it was through man that Allah was able to see and contemplate Himself through the creation of this creature, but He has to blow the ruh into this creature so that the unpolished mirror could become polished and have light.

"Then we must speak of the container. The container proceeds from none other than His most sacredly pure overflowing."

He is saying that the created creature, man, comes from the most sacred Essence of Allah, subhanahu wa ta'ala, and yet he is now, in the universe, the creature with a ruh.

"So the whole affair has its beginning from Allah and its end is to Him and the whole affair will return to Him as it began from Him. Thus the command decreed the polishing of the mirror of the universe, and Adam was the very polishing of that mirror, and the ruh of that form.

"Tajalli only comes from the Essence by means of the forms of predisposition of the one to whom the Tajalli is made," in other words, the container. The Tajalli from the Essence only comes because man has been created for this. He is predisposed to receive this event. "The one who receives the Tajalli will only see his own form in the mirror of the Real, and he will not see the Real for it is not possible to see Him."

Sayyiduna Musa, 'alayhi salam, said, "I want to see You," and Allah said, "You cannot see Me but look at the mountain," and the mountain crumbled to pieces and he then received this Divine knowledge by his own fana'.

"At the same time he knows that he sees only his own form in it. It is like the mirror in the visible world – inasmuch as you see forms in it, or your own form, you do not see the mirror." If you look at the mirror you do not see the mirror, you see yourself. "At the same time you know that you see the forms or your form only by virtue of the mirror. Allah manifests this as a mithal," this is an essential part of the human creature, "appropriate to the Tajalli of His Essence, so that the one receiving the Tajalli knows that he does not see Him."

Thus when Allah manifests to him he does not see Him, he sees himself. "Man 'arafa nafsahu fa qad 'arafa Rabbah." He who knows himself knows his Lord.

"There is no mithal nearer and more appropriate to vision and Tajalli than this, so try in yourself when you see the form in the mirror to see the body of the mirror as well – you will never do it. If you wish to taste of this, then experience the limit beyond which there is no higher limit possible in respect to the creature. Neither aspire, nor tire yourself in going beyond this degree for in principle there is only pure non-existence after it. Allah is then your mirror in which you see yourself, and you are His mirror in which He sees His Names."

This returns us to our primary understanding of the difference between the Divine Essence and the essences of created things. We look at the Diwan of Shaykh Muhammad ibn al-Habib, radiyallahu 'anhu, in the qasida 'Withdrawal from all that is other-than-Allah':

نُـورُ الإلَـهِ فَـلا تَـرَى إلاَّهُ   رُوحِي تُحَدِّثُنِـي بِـأنَّ حَقِيقَتِي

إنَّ السِّوَا عَـدَمٌ فَـلا تَرْضَاهُ   لَوْ لَمْ أكُـنْ نُوراً لَكُنْتُ سِواهُ

غَيْرَ الإلَـهِ فِي أرْضِـهِ وَسَماهُ   وَإذا نَظَرْتَ بِعَيْنِ سِرِّكَ لَمْ تَجِدْ

فَأنْبُـذْ هَواكَ إذا أرَدْتَ تَراهُ   لَكِنْ تَوَهُّمُ غَيْرِهِ يَخْفَـى بِــهِ

My ruh speaks to me and says,
"My Haqiqat is the Light of Allah,
so look to no-one except Him.

If I were not a light I would be other-than-Him.
Indeed otherness is nothingness
so do not be content with it.

If you look with the eye of your Secret," the inner eye,
"you will not find a trace of other-than-Allah
in either earth or heaven.

But the illusion of other-than-Him hides Him.
So combat your desires if you wish to see Him."

In other words, rise above this nafs that insists on the reality of things and does not realise the secret which is that if you look with the eye of your Secret you will not find anything that is other-than-Allah.

Thus from the stand-point of created forms everything is masiwallah. From the point of view of the forms brought into existence everything is other-than-Allah. But from the inward aspect, all things are His from before-time and after it. "If I were not a light I would be other-than-Him. Otherness is nothingness so do not be content with it. If you look with the eye of your Secret you will not find a trace of other-than-Allah in either earth or heaven."

We will now look at Surat an-Nahl (16:96) for the final clarification of this matter, confirming what I have said. This ayat is astonishing:

$$\text{مَا عِندَكُمْ يَنفَدُ وَمَا عِندَ اللَّهِ بَاقٍ}$$

What is with you runs out,
but what is with Allah goes on forever.

There is an in-time aspect of you which runs out and then that is it, finished and gone. But in the secret, what is with Allah goes on forever. The reality is that the Essence is present so you are in the knowledge of Allah. You have come into the creation and He is the Knower, and then when you are finished you return to Him, there is the Judgment Day and all the unfolding of the secrets of the Malakut. You go from the Mulk to the Malakut to the Jabarut to the meeting with the Essence because you have been known to Allah, subhanahu wa ta'ala, before the creation of the world.

In Qur'an we know very well the ayat where Allah orders all of mankind before the creation of the world in the Essence – in His knowledge, the 'Alim – and says to them, in Surat al-A'raf (7:172):

$$\text{أَلَسْتُ بِرَبِّكُمْ}$$

Am I not your Lord?

and all the human creatures say,

$$\text{قَالُوا بَلَىٰ شَهِدْنَا}$$

We testify that indeed You are!

Then Allah, by the Command, puts them into the world in their time and in their place, and Allah says in Surat al-'Ankabut (29:2):

$$\text{أَحَسِبَ النَّاسُ أَنْ يُتْرَكُوا}$$
$$\text{أَنْ يَقُولُوا آمَنَّا وَهُمْ لَا يُفْتَنُونَ ۝}$$

Do people imagine that they will be left to say, 'We have iman,' and will not be tested?

So they are tested and you see who are this and you see who are that. You see who are the muminun and you see who are the kafirun, and you see in between who are the munafiqun. Then they will be gathered to Allah, sub-hanahu wa ta'ala.

"What is with you runs out but what is with Allah goes on forever." "What is with you runs out," ends with the washing of the body and the funeral prayer. "What is with Allah goes on forever," is the fulfilment of the meaning of the life when the form of the life has been returned to its Owner in the earth and the phosphates have gone to the phosphates and the potassium has gone to the potassium and the minerals have returned to the earth. Then what is with Allah goes on forever, some for the Fire and some for the Garden. Allah, subhanahu wa ta'ala, says: "I send some to the Fire and I do not care, I send some to the Garden and I do not care," because this is part of the Divine unfolding of the Essence of Allah, subhanahu wa ta'ala, and this is the reality of the Haqq and this is the One Whom we worship and we associate nothing with Him.

Fatiha.

REFLECTION

from the Diwan of Shaykh Muhammad ibn al-Habib

رَائِيَّةُ التَّفْكِيرِ

تَفَكَّرْ جَمِيلَ الصُّنْعِ فِي الْبَرِّ وَالْبَحْرِ   وَجُلْ فِي صِفَاتِ اللهِ فِي السِّرِّ وَالْجَهْرِ

وَفِي النَّفْسِ وَالْآفَاقِ أَعْظَمُ شَاهِدٍ   عَلَى كَمَالَاتِ اللهِ مِنْ غَيْرِ مَا حَصْرِ

فَلَوْ جُلْتَ فِي الْأَجْسَامِ مَعْ حُسْنِ شَكْلِهَا   وَتَنْظِيمِهَا تَنْظِيمَ خَيْطٍ مِنَ الدُّرِّ

وَجُلْتَ فِي أَسْرَارِ اللِّسَانِ وَنُطْقِهِ   وَتَعْبِيرِهِ عَمَّا تُكِنُّهُ فِي الصَّدْرِ

وَجُلْتَ فِي أَسْرَارِ الْجَوَارِحِ كُلِّهَا   وَتَسْخِيرِهَا لِلْقَلْبِ مِنْ غَيْرِ مَا عُسْرِ

وَجُلْتَ فِي تَقْلِيبِ الْقُلُوبِ لِطَاعَةٍ   وَفِي بَعْضِ أَحْيَانٍ لِمَعْصِيَةٍ تَسْرِي

وَجُلْتَ فِي أَرْضٍ مَعْ تَنَوُّعِ نَبْتِهَا   وَكَثْرَةِ مَا فِيهَا مِنَ السَّهْلِ وَالْوَعْرِ

وَجُلْتَ فِي أَسْرَارِ الْبِحَارِ وَحُوتِهَا   وَكَثْرَةِ أَمْوَاجٍ لَهَا حَاجِزٌ قَهْرِ

وَجُلْتَ فِي أَسْرَارِ الرِّيَاحِ وَجَلْبِهَا   لِغَيْمٍ وَسُحْبٍ قَدْ أَسَالَتْ مِنَ الْقَطْرِ

وَجُلْتَ فِي أَسْرَارِ السَّمَوَاتِ كُلِّهَا   وَعَرْشٍ وَكُرْسِيٍّ وَرُوحٍ مِنَ الْأَمْرِ

عَقَدْتَ عَلَى التَّوْحِيدِ عَقْدَ مُصَمِّمٍ   وَحُلْتَ عَنِ الْأَوْهَامِ وَالشَّكِّ وَالْغَيْرِ

وَقُلْتَ إِلَاهِي أَنْتَ سُؤْلِي وَمَطْلَبِي   وَحِصْنِي مِنَ الْأَسْوَاءِ وَالضَّيْمِ وَالْمَكْرِ

وَأَنْتَ رَجَائِي فِي قَضَاءِ حَوَائِجِي   وَأَنْتَ الَّذِي تُنْجِي مِنَ السُّوءِ وَالشَّرِّ

وَأَنْتَ الرَّحِيمُ الْمُسْتَجِيبُ لِمَنْ دَعَاكْ   وَأَنْتَ الَّذِي تُغْنِي الْفَقِيرَ عَنِ الْفَقْرِ

إِلَيْكَ رَفَعْتُ يَا رَفِيعُ مَطَالِبِي   فَعَجِّلْ بِفَتْحٍ يَا إِلَاهِي مَعَ السِّرِّ

بِجَاهِ الَّذِي يُرْجَى يَوْمَ الْكَرْبِ وَالْعَنَا   وَيَوْمَ وُرُودِ النَّاسِ لِمَوْقِفِ الْحَشْرِ

عَلَيْهِ صَلَاةُ اللهِ مَا جَالَ عَارِفٌ   فِي أَنْوَارِ ذَاتِهِ لَدَى كُلِّ مَظْهَرِ

وَآلِهِ وَالْأَصْحَابِ مَعْ كُلِّ تَابِعٍ   لِسُنَّتِهِ الْغَرَّاءِ فِي النَّهْيِ وَالْأَمْرِ

Reflect upon the beauty of the way in which both the land and sea are made, and contemplate the Attributes of Allah outwardly and secretly.

The greatest evidence of the limitless perfections of Allah can be found both deep within the self and on the distant horizon.

If you were to reflect on physical bodies and their marvellous forms and how they are arranged with great precision, like a string of pearls,

And if you were to reflect on the secrets of the tongue and its capacity for speech, and how it articulates and conveys what you conceal in your breast,

And if you were to reflect on the secrets of all the limbs and how easily they are subject to the heart's command,

And if you were to reflect on how the hearts are moved to obey Allah and how at other times they move darkly to disobedience,

And if you were to reflect on the earth and the diversity of its plants and the great varieties of smooth and rugged land in it,

And if you were to reflect on the secrets of the oceans and all their fish, and their endless waves held back by an unconquerable barrier,

And if you were to reflect on the secrets of the many

winds and how they bring the mist, fog and clouds which release the rain,

And if you were to reflect on all the secrets of the heavens – the Throne and the Footstool and the spirit sent by the Command –

Then you would accept the reality of Tawhid with all your being, and you would turn away from illusions, uncertainty and otherness,

And you would say, "My God, You are my desire, my goal and my impregnable fortress against evil, injustice and deceit.

You are the One I hope will provide for all my needs, and You are the One Who rescues us from all evil and wickedness.

You are the Compassionate, the One Who answers all who call on You. And you are the One Who enriches the poverty of the faqir.

It is to You, O Exalted, that I have raised all my request, so swiftly bring me the Opening, the rescue and the secret, O my God."

By the rank of the one in whom we hope on the day of distress and grief – that terrible day when people come to the Place of Gathering –

May Allah's blessings by upon him as long as there is an

'Arif who reflects on the lights of His Essence in every manifestation,

And upon his family and Companions and everyone who follows his excellent Sunna in all its prohibitions and commands.

HADRA

We ask Allah, subhanahu wa ta'ala, to keep us in the company of the 'Arifin. We ask Allah, subhanahu wa ta'ala, to let the people of this dhikr spread out through the whole of Africa and take the Deen to all of Africa. We ask Allah, subhanahu wa ta'ala, to give to Africa the Deen of Islam that has been rejected by the Arabs. We ask Allah, subhanahu wa ta'ala, to give baraka to the people of this room.

We ask Allah, subhanahu wa ta'ala, to make the people of this room people of baraka, people of wisdom and people of teaching. We ask Allah, subhanahu wa ta'ala, to give benefit to all the people who see the fuqara and meet the fuqara so that they love them and respect them.